I Just Hope It's Lethal

Poems of Sadness, Madness, and Joy

Collected by LIZ ROSENBERG & DEENA NOVEMBER

An Imprint of Houghton Mifflin Company

Boston 2005

Compilation copyright © 2005 by Liz Rosenberg and Deena November
Introduction © 2005 by Liz Rosenberg. Introduction © 2005 by Deena November

www.houghtonmifflinbooks.com

The text of this book is set in Rotis Serif.

Library of Congress Cataloging-in-Publication Data
is on file

LCCN 2005004257

ISBN-13: 978-0618-56452-1

Manufactured in the United States of America

HAD 10 9 8 7 6 5 4 3 2 1

A list of permissions appears on pages 178–82.

With grateful thanks to our editors, Judy O'Malley and Eden Edwards, and for the able assistance of Erica Zappy. Thanks forever to my husband, David; and to our son, Eli, and daughter, Lily, our own Prozac nation. This book is for all who suffer, fall, and rise: you are not alone. —LMR

To my family and friends for putting up with me and my many alarm clocks. —DN

CONTENTS

INTRODUCTION

Deena November

I haven't been out of my teenage years for that long now, but I will always remember them whether I want to or not. Life is insane, the world is insane, and this is nothing new nor profound. Tragically, being a teenager makes everything feel much worse. Adults mock the "no one understands me" aspect that we know and live all too well.

When I was in my early teens, I was convinced I would surely die before I reached twenty, either naturally or self-induced. There were times I felt alienated, misunderstood, and depressed. Once, I threw a wooden chair at my mother out of frustration. All through high school I was crying in detention, contemplating walking into traffic, and rescheduling appointments with my therapist in between classes. I didn't want to be living a life I couldn't exist in anymore.

Feeling unmotivated, trapped, unheard, and suicidal, I began to take pictures, draw, and, most passionately, to write. I found writing to be an outlet for my depression, and it has been my savior ever since. I only hope that everyone who has ever experienced days that seem like hell finds some sort of creative outlet that sparks a passion and motivation to wake up, take a shower, and live out each day.

The poems in this book have been selected to convey the emotions, thoughts, and tribulations of poets throughout time. I wish that this book had existed when I was going through the insanity of love, aggravation, depression, and the disappointments of being misunderstood by adults and fellow teens during my teenage years.

When I was in high school, my classmates found it difficult to understand me as I sank deeper into my own depression. "If you only smile and pretend to be happy then you will become happy" was my principal's advice. I wish it were that simple. But that's not how it works, unfortunately.

What has helped many of my friends and me has been reading about others' struggles with life. People need to know they aren't crazy or mad just because they are depressed or because they feel anxious streaks of insanity drive them. Teenagers especially need to hear that many people throughout history and around the world experienced depression, and that it's fairly common.

This book is for everyone and anyone. The poems collected here offer a better understanding of those people who know what it's like to never want to wake up in the morning or those who can't pacify racing thoughts. Liz Rosenberg and I offer you this anthology as a way of coping with life and the struggle to find balance. We give you a book of poets who live or have lived with these problems and found some comfort in their writing.

When I feel like crawling out of my own body and mind, I read or write. By reading about others' experiences with depression, I know I'm not the only one struggling and that there are ways to return to a real smile without having to pretend.

INTRODUCTION

Liz Rosenberg

The idea for this book came about through a project that Deena began in a creative writing class at the State University of New York at Binghamton, a collection of favorite poems. When Deena showed me the title, *I Just Hope It's Lethal*, I laughed out loud. It may take a fellow sufferer to appreciate the joke of that title.

Deena and I had worked together as student and teacher. I had taught her brother Josh, another gifted poet, in earlier classes. I knew Deena struggled with depression. She knew I had suffered in many similar ways. When I saw that Deena had gathered a dozen poems about various aspects of sanity or madness, I thought it could make a wonderful book for young readers.

When I was a teenager, I combed my school library for the few books that spoke to my own up-and-down experience of the world, and I lit upon writers such as Sylvia Plath, Robert Lowell, Stevie Smith, and John Berryman with hungry gratitude. I was not alone with what I felt. If the way ahead was something of a swamp at times, at least here were footprints, proof that others had traveled this path.

Initially, Deena and I had thought we'd try to find about fifty poems for the book—instead we found close to one hundred. Deena took responsibility for obtaining author permissions—a daunting task for someone so young. I took on the bulk of the poet biographies and chipped away at them little by little. After our original editor, Judy O'Malley, left Houghton Mifflin, Eden Edwards took on the project with warmth and affection, and helped us to further refine the book.

We decided to divide it into five sections. The first would deal mainly with moods—what my teenage son sometimes calls "sadness without reason." There is a Portuguese word, *sowdadge*, for that mood. But there are other moods and frames of mind without names—feeling like a stranger on the earth, feeling unreasonable joy, rebellion, disquiet, restlessness. We thought that poems about a wide range of moods, which nearly everyone experiences at one time or another, would make a good introduction to a book that addresses the whole notion of "sanity" and "insanity," and the sometimes fine line that divides them.

Next came a section about being crazy in love—a temporary derangement common to all, but especially achingly keen in youth.

We wanted a section that addressed ways in which the world itself can be deranged. Poets make it their business to show the insanity of war, of inequity, cruelty, false ambitions, and false dreams. There are certain circumstances in which being "insane" is in fact the only way to remain truly sane.

We also needed a section dedicated to poems by poets who clearly identify a period of insanity. Poets write often about madness, and as their biographies prove, they are vulnerable to bouts of insanity in their own lives. Writers from

Shakespeare to Dickinson have described madness—some poets rendering it comically, others giving it the darkest and most intense seriousness.

Finally, there is the relief of coming up out of a bad period. We call this section "Wish You Were Here," evoking a postcard one sends from a beautiful and exotic place. While you are still stumbling around, or falling in darkness, it's hard to believe things will ever feel, look, or even taste better. But, as the poet Jane Kenyon and others show us, the way out of despair can be long and difficult, but it is almost certain. One must be patient and brave.

Deena and I come from different generations. At the start, we assumed we would bring entirely different tastes and poems to this collection. We both think this is a richer collection than either one of us could have come to alone, but our tastes proved remarkably similar.

For me, this book has been an amazing journey through a landscape at once strange and familiar. I was seventeen, a teenager myself, when I first recognized my own depression and began to seek treatment and help. It's been a long, sometimes agonizing journey—like struggling with some mighty demon—but because of it I have forged deep friendships and alliances along the way. "To sing was the only way through," wrote poet Milton Kessler. Poetry can help us survive. We hope this book will be a guide for those who find themselves lost in a dark wilderness. We know for some readers it will simply be an interesting group of poems linked by a common theme, with many variations. It is remarkable how the voices seem to call back and forth across cultures and ages.

This book was a double blessing for me, because for the first time I edited an anthology of poems with a collaborator—a fellow traveler. Deena and I bowed to one another's passions and peculiarities. We could not in the end print every poem we loved, or every poem that seemed to belong. One always makes hard choices in editing an anthology—it was a bit easier to make those choices with a partner. Only now, once the book is in the hands of the reader, is the journey really complete.

Sadness Without Reason:

MOODS

A SAD CHILD

by Margaret Atwood

You're sad because you're sad.
It's psychic. It's the age. It's chemical.
Go see a shrink or take a pill,
or hug your sadness like an eyeless doll
you need to sleep.

Well, all children are sad
but some get over it.
Count your blessings. Better than that,
buy a hat. Buy a coat or pet.
Take up dancing to forget.

Forget what?
Your sadness, your shadow,
whatever it was that was done to you
the day of the lawn party
when you came inside flushed with the sun,
your mouth sulky with sugar,
in your new dress with the ribbon
and the ice-cream smear,
and said to yourself in the bathroom,
I am not the favourite child.

My darling, when it comes
right down to it
and the light fails and the fog rolls in
and you're trapped in your overturned body
under a blanket or burning car,

and the red flame is seeping out of you
and igniting the tarmac beside your head
or else the floor, or else the pillow,
none of us is;
or else we all are.

■ ■ ■

INFANT SORROW

by William Blake

My mother groaned, my father wept—
Into the dangerous world I leapt,
Helpless, naked, piping loud,
Like a fiend hid in a cloud.

Struggling in my father's hands,
Striving against my swaddling bands,
Bound and weary, I thought best
To sulk upon my mother's breast.

■■■

I HATE MY MOANING

by Gerald Stern

I hate my staring. I hate my moaning. Sometimes
I lie there in the morning arguing
against myself. I hold a mirror up
above the telephone so I can snip
a long hair from my eye. I balance a cup
of coffee on my stomach. Sometimes I sing,
sometimes I hold a feather against my nose,
sometimes I prop the clock against my ear,
sometimes I drag the speakers across the floor
and turn the volume up. There is a hole
above my head, the plaster is dropping, the lath
is exposed; there is a blanket over the window;
I hold it up with nails, it tears in the center
and lets a stream of light in; I can tell
when it's six o'clock, and seven o'clock, it is
my hour, the blanket is full of holes, the light
comes through the threads, it is a greyish light,
perfect for either love or bitterness,
no exaggeration or deceit.

■ ■ ■

"I LIKE MY ANGER MY GROUCHY FURIOUS LOVE"

by Ikkyū
Translated by Stephen Berg

I like my anger my grouchy furious love
amazing how we say such nice things about the dead

■ ■ ■

THE STRANGER

by Charles Baudelaire

Translated by Louise Varèse

Tell me, enigmatical man, whom do you love best, your father, your mother, your sister, or your brother?

I have neither father, nor mother, nor sister, nor brother.

Your friends?

Now you use a word whose meaning I have never known.

Your country?

I do not know in what latitude it lies.

Beauty?

I could indeed love her, Goddess and Immortal.

Gold?

I hate it as you hate God.

Then, what do you love, extraordinary stranger?

I love the clouds . . . the clouds that pass . . . up there . . . up there . . . the wonderful clouds!

■ ■ ■

A PLACE FOR EVERYTHING

by Louis Jenkins

It's so easy to lose track of things. A screwdriver, for instance. "Where did I put that? I had it in my hand just a minute ago." You wander vaguely from room to room, having forgotten, by now, what you were looking for, staring into the refrigerator, the bathroom mirror . . . "I really could use a shave. . . ."

Some objects seem to disappear immediately while others never want to leave. Here is a small black plastic gizmo with a serious demeanor that turns up regularly, like a politician at public functions. It seems to be an "integral part," a kind of switch with screw holes so that it can be attached to something larger. Nobody knows what. This thing's use has been forgotten but it looks so important that no one is willing to throw it in the trash. It survives by bluff, like certain insects that escape being eaten because of their formidable appearance.

My father owned a large, three-bladed, brass propeller that he saved for years. Its worth was obvious, it was just that it lacked an immediate application since we didn't own a boat and lived hundreds of miles from any large bodies of water. The propeller survived all purges and cleanings, living, like royalty, a life of lonely privilege, mounted high on the garage wall.

■■■

A LARGER LONELINESS

by Eli Bosnick

One lone tree
is drinking God's silence.

■■■

THE EYES OF MY REGRET

by Angelina Weld Grimké

Always at dusk, the same tearless experience,
The same dragging of feet up the same well-worn path
To the same well-worn rock;
The same crimson or gold dropping away of the sun,
The same tints—rose, saffron, violet, lavender, grey,
Meeting, mingling, mixing mistily;
Before me the same blue black cedar rising jaggedly
      to a point;
Over it, the same slow unlidding of twin stars,
Two eyes unfathomable, soul-searing,
Watching, watching—watching me;
The same two eyes that draw me forth, against my will dusk
      after dusk;
The same two eyes that keep me sitting late into the night,
      chin on knees,
Keep me there lonely, rigid, tearless, numbly miserable,
      —The eyes of my Regret.

■ ■ ■

LET NO CHARITABLE HOPE

by Elinor Wylie

Now let no charitable hope
Confuse my mind with images
Of eagle and of antelope:
I am in nature none of these.

I was, being human, born alone;
I am, being woman, hard beset;
I live by squeezing from a stone
The little nourishment I get.

In masks outrageous and austere
The years go by in single file;
But none has merited my fear,
And none has quite escaped my smile.

■ ■ ■

"A WHITE CITY"

by Michael Burkard

In the dream, N. is singing "a white city." A teacher he had is wearing a girdle wider than a wide tree. The teacher is from years ago. The teacher led the children singing a wretched song of "Trees." Now the dream is altering the song, and N. is laughing as he stops singing "the white city" and begins singing "I think that I shall never see / a girdle large as this old tree." He awakes, laughing hysterically. He remembers in the morning Mrs. G., the teacher, her hatchet face, her black hair high, her sweaters and skirts of lime and black and violet. N. goes out to buy a morning paper and is more than shocked to read that Mrs. G. has died the day before.

N.'s life has been rapidly dissolving for a year because of alcohol. He has lost much. The dream has distracted him from this momentarily—the amount of laughter has (for there has been little, it seems, to laugh about)—and now this, the obituary.

The death, the dream, trees. The giving to him with begrudgment the collection of her son's sports scrapbooks, though she had urged someone in the class to take these off her hands at the end of the school year. She was "cleaning house."

And N.'s awkwardness, walking the two miles home with them the final day of school, dropping pieces from them again and again, stopping, stooping. The end of the year, the long time, and now this.

■ ■ ■

"DO YOU THINK I KNOW WHAT I'M DOING?"

by Rumi

Translated by Coleman Barks

Do you think I know what I'm doing?
That for one breath or half-breath I belong to myself?
As much as a pen knows what it's writing,
or the ball can guess where it's going next.

■ ■ ■

TO SOLITUDE

by John Keats

O Solitude! if I must with thee dwell,
    Let it not be among the jumbled heap
    Of murky buildings; climb with me the steep,—
Nature's observatory—whence the dell,
Its flowery slopes, its river's crystal swell,
    May seem a span; let me thy vigils keep
    'Mongst boughs pavillion'd, where the deer's swift leap
Startles the wild bee from the fox-glove bell.
But though I'll gladly trace these scenes with thee,
    Yet the sweet converse of an innocent mind,
    Whose words are images of thoughts refin'd,
Is my soul's pleasure; and it sure must be
    Almost the highest bliss of human-kind,
When to thy haunts two kindred spirits flee.

■ ■ ■

REALITY'S DARK DREAM

by Samuel Taylor Coleridge

I know 'tis but a dream, yet feel more anguish
Than if 'twere truth. It has been often so:
Must I die under it? Is no one near?
Will no one hear these stifled groans and wake me?

■ ■ ■

END OF WINTER

by Liz Rosenberg

The pine tree shivers like a match flame
     in the last black snows of April.
The birds came back too soon from Florida
where last week they saw: hot-pink hibiscus! palm trees!
egrets walking smoothly, like Egyptian gods.

We'd better take this world as we find it:
Through three panes of glass enough beauty
comes sifting down
to make a sane person happy,
or a sad one sane.
Tenderly I wrap the dead black fly in a white sheet of tissue,
who lay so many days on my attic sill.
As I carry him downstairs, I feel his life humming
     between my fingers,
before I flush him away. May someone, someday,
     be as gentle with me.

■ ■ ■

RICHARD CORY

by Edwin Arlington Robinson

Whenever Richard Cory went down town,
We people on the pavement looked at him:
He was a gentleman from sole to crown,
Clean favored, and imperially slim.

And he was always quietly arrayed,
And he was always human when he talked;
But still he fluttered pulses when he said,
"Good-morning," and he glittered when he walked.

And he was rich, — yes, richer than a king, —
And admirably schooled in every grace:
In fine, we thought that he was everything
To make us wish that we were in his place.

So on we worked, and waited for the light,
And went without the meat, and cursed the bread;
And Richard Cory, one calm summer night,
Went home and put a bullet through his head.

■■■

NOT WAVING BUT DROWNING

by Stevie Smith

Nobody heard him, the dead man,
But still he lay moaning:
I was much further out than you thought
And not waving but drowning.

Poor chap, he always loved larking
And now he's dead
It must have been too cold for him his heart gave way,
They said.

Oh, no no no, it was too cold always
(Still the dead one lay moaning)
I was much too far out all my life
And not waving but drowning.

■■■

Wild
WORLD

SYMPATHY

by Paul Laurence Dunbar

I know what the caged bird feels, alas!
     When the sun is bright on the upland slopes;
When the wind stirs soft through the springing grass,
And the river flows like a stream of glass;
     When the first bird sings and the first bud opes,
And the faint perfume from its chalice steals—
I know what the caged bird feels!

I know why the caged bird beats his wing
     Till its blood is red on the cruel bars;
For he must fly back to his perch and cling
When he fain would be on the bough a-swing;
     And a pain still throbs in the old, old scars
And they pulse again with a keener sting—
I know why he beats his wing!

I know why the caged bird sings, ah me,
     When his wing is bruised and his bosom sore,—
When he beats his bars and he would be free;
It is not a carol of joy or glee,
     But a prayer that he sends from his heart's deep core,
But a plea, that upward to Heaven he flings—
I know why the caged bird sings!

■ ■ ■

""MUCH MADNESS IS DIVINEST SENSE"

by Emily Dickinson

Much Madness is divinest Sense—
To a discerning Eye—
Much Sense—the starkest Madness—
'Tis the Majority
In this, as All, prevail—
Assent—and you are sane—
Demur—you're straightway dangerous—
And handled with a Chain—

■ ■ ■

From YOU ARE OLD, FATHER WILLIAM

by Lewis Carroll

"You are old, Father William," the young man said
    "And your hair has become very white;
And yet you incessantly stand on your head—
    Do you think, at your age, it is right?"

"In my youth," Father William replied to his son,
    "I feared it might injure the brain;
But, now that I'm perfectly sure I have none,
    Why, I do it again and again."

"You are old," said the youth, "as I mentioned before.
    And have grown most uncommonly fat;
Yet you turned a back-somersault in at the door—
    Pray, what is the reason of that?"

"In my youth," said the sage, as he shook his grey locks,
    "I kept all my limbs very supple
By the use of this ointment—one shilling the box—
    Allow me to sell you a couple?"

■ ■ ■

LONDON

by William Blake

I wander thro' each charter'd street,
Near where the charter'd Thames does flow,
And mark in every face I meet
Marks of weakness, marks of woe.

In every cry of every Man,
In every Infants cry of fear,
In every voice, in every ban,
The mind-forg'd manacles I hear

How the Chimney-sweepers cry
Every blackning Church appalls,
And the hapless Soldiers sigh
Runs in blood down Palace walls

But most thro' midnight streets I hear
How the youthful Harlots curse
Blasts the new-born Infants tear
And blights with plagues the Marriage hearse

■ ■ ■

HOLDING THE HOLY CARD

by J. Patrick Lewis

They've got me down as manic.
Or is it up as manic?
Or is it down as fifteen years of panic?
Words beat the crap out of me—
flat liner, pharmacy bait, no tickety-boo,
lights on, nobody home.

Jude Thaddeus, patron saint
of lost causes, talk to me.
Clubbed to death in the first century.
Says so on the back of your halo snapshot
that will forever touch my skin.
Has to touch it, can't stop touching it,
or . . . , or what?
You wouldn't believe me if I told you.

But what I'd like to know is this,
among all the bogus believers—
hucksters, healers, psychics—
what's wrong with one more rabbit's foot
hiding in my holy hocus pocus armory
of charms against the zoned-out articles
of faith we swear to?

■ ■ ■

ODA PARA LETICIA

by Oscar Bermeo

Leticia, no sé como decir lo que estoy pensando.
Words have failed to live up to my expectations.
What I have to say is so basic.
Something I have done a hundred times before.
How will you receive these words?
This thought leaves me uncomfortable.

Si tan sólo pudieras decírmelo en
Español en nuestro idioma.
Tus ojos brillan con la frustración
De estar atrapado en el lenguaje que te crió,
Que te enseño una madrastra que te dio todo
Lo que tienes
Menos el cariño de la cuna.

If I did know my heritage this might feel right
So proud I have been of being Ecuadorian.
Now, I feel I know nothing of who I am,
where I'm from, where we are from, Leticia.
If only you knew English, knew the winters of New York.
Then you might understand
how Castellano
becomes Spanish,
slips into English,
bastardly reclaimed as Spanglish.
How we fight to hold on to who we are

¿Acaso nuanca te contaron tu historia?
¿Acaso tu padre no te enseño el escuda de familia? ,
¿Acaso tu madre no te cantó en la cuna?
¿Acaso tu abuela no te ayudó a descubrir tu identidad
contándote cuentos de sus antepasados?

I have never heard the tales of my family.
Not who we really are.
Ma would chastise abuela;
"Mami, if you keep feeding them *tus cuentos*
how will they stand a chance?"
but if we don't know who we are
how can we stand at all?

Dime lo que me quieres decir.
Quiero oír tus palabras.
Puras, de tu boca, libres de traducción
Sentir donde estás
Darme cuenta adonde quieres llegar.

It sounds simple when you say it.
That we can cross
These miles that separate us
With some common phrase, used before
Without thought or
Fear of consequence.
Not these words,
So much will go into what I will say
These words can never be invalidated.
These words will always mean something.

Olvida el pasado y sus limitaciones
Con lengua quebrada,
Háblame del alma. . . .

'Yo sé lo que te quiero decir, pero no sé las palabras
y eso es lo más importante para mí.
Que tú entiendas mis sentimientos
que sepas de mi, mi . . .'
that you know exactly what I mean.
I will not use a phrase plucked from the sky
just to satisfy this moment. Not
      "Te aprecio"
When I mean to say thank you for making
me feel wanted here, where I was born?
I've waited so long to feel strangely like this.
So how can I show my appreciation
with just two simple words?
or even with one?
      "Gracias"
These words don't seem enough.

Entiendo tus sentimientos y
Sé que la distancia es mucha más
que este aire que está entre nosotros.
Es el espacio en la mente
que se atreve a separarnos.
Cálmate, m'ijo,
puedes estar seguro aquí—en tu hogar

Leticia, I need you to know
How hard I have fought
So you can receive
the spirit of these words.

■ ■ ■

clean that god damned room already

by Deena November

every mess i made is mine
starting with my lies
ending with my going to bed
and waking up two days later
cramped and sore at 21 years old

surrounded by maroon nylon bags
filled with clean clothes
claiming my dirty bedroom floor
that i refuse to vacuum
not even for myself

so, i'm forced to pick up crumbs
with my bare feet
not by choice of course
my feet just happen to absorb the mess
i'm the author to all my life

■ ■ ■

HER KIND

by Anne Sexton

I have gone out, a possessed witch,
haunting the black air, braver at night;
dreaming evil, I have done my hitch
over the plain houses, light by light:
lonely thing, twelve-fingered, out of mind.
A woman like that is not a woman, quite.
I have been her kind.

I have found the warm caves in the woods,
filled them with skillets, carvings, shelves,
closets, silks, innumerable goods;
fixed the suppers for the worms and the elves:
whining, rearranging the disaligned.
A woman like that is misunderstood.
I have been her kind.

I have ridden in your cart, driver,
waved my nude arms at villages going by,
learning the last bright routes, survivor
where your flames still bite my thigh
and my ribs crack where your wheels wind.
A woman like that is not ashamed to die.
I have been her kind.

■ ■ ■

ORNATE IRON GATES

by Das Lanzilloti

The ornate iron gates
      closed off the world
locked with a thunderous clank
as billows of acrid dust
      rose in shafts of sunlight
in the dark corridors of the asylum.
Breathing in the darkness and the hopelessness
you walk on cold tile floors
in a Thorazine daze
then another door is locked behind you
this is the door to your room
a tiny window with rusted bars
a slant of sunbeam penetrates the dark
every day at 3:05 PM and stays until 3:22 PM
then it's gone until tomorrow
unless of course the sun doesn't shine.
The gouged paint, the pounded walls
are testimony to someone's anger
someone who occupied this room before
they're gone but their anger stayed behind.
Thursdays and Tuesdays and Sundays and dates
all dissolve into each other
all seen through the rusty bars
while the hideous green walls
strangle your heart and your spirit.

Tomorrow is evaluation day
the board of lunatic doctors
will determine whether or not
you've regained your sanity
whether or not you can be reunited
with the lunatic hordes
beyond the ornate iron gates . . .

■ ■ ■

From THE BLACK RIDERS AND OTHER LINES

by Stephen Crane

3

In the desert
I saw a creature, naked, bestial,
Who, squatting upon the ground,
Held his heart in his hands,
And ate of it.
I said: "Is it good, friend?"
"It is bitter—bitter," he answered;
"But I like it
Because it is bitter,
And because it is my heart."

7

Mystic shadow, bending near me,
Who art thou?
Whence come ye?
And—tell me—is it fair
Or is the truth bitter as eaten fire?
Tell me!
Fear not that I should quaver,
For I dare—I dare.
Then, tell me!

24

I saw a man pursuing the horizon;
Round and round they sped.
I was disturbed at this;
I accosted the man.
"It is futile," I said,
"You can never—"

"You lie," he cried,
And ran on.

47

"Think as I think," said a man,
"Or you are abominably wicked;
You are a toad."

And after I had thought of it,
I said: "I will, then, be a toad."

57

With eye and with gesture
You say you are holy.
I say you lie;
For I did see you
Draw away your coats
From the sin upon the hands
Of a little child.
Liar!

65

Once, I knew a fine song,
—It is true, believe me,—
It was all of birds,
And I held them in a basket;
When I opened the wicket,
Heavens! they all flew away.
I cried: "Come back, little thoughts!"
But they only laughed.
They flew on
Until they were as sand
Thrown between me and the sky.

■ ■ ■

KITCHEN

by Twain Dooley

Ring-a-ding-a-ding, school bell a ring,
knife and fork a fight fi dumplin

—Shabba Ranks

Everywhere I go it's the same old thing
Spoons are always stirring up something
Always in Knife and Fork's business

Talking about how Knife ain't cutting it no more
And Fork's gone poking around on his own
It's getting hot

Equal is busy trying to take Sugar's place
Broom is talking about how Vacuum sucks
It's getting hot

Pot just called Kettle a racial slur
But it's cool since they are of the same ethnic origin
Right?

Something fishy is going on in the trash
I swear at any moment T-Pot's gonna blow the whistle
It's getting hot

Something funky is going on in the refrigerator
Jell-O's over there trying to play it cool
But we all know how shaky he is

Ice thinks he's cool, hard, slick
But there's a whole rack of fools just like him
Locked up in the deep freeze (bunch of squares)

Some may laugh
They live plush living room lives
I grew up on the hard cold linoleum of the kitchen

Where it's getting too hot
And I can't find my way out

■ ■ ■

IN THE BOOBIEHATCH

by Das Lanzilloti

in the boobiehatch
the only difference
between the crazies
and the staff
is the colour of the shirts
those of the crazies are grey
and those of the staff are blue
except for that
there is no difference
that i can see
between the crazies and the staff

■ ■ ■

AUTUMN BEGINS IN
MARTINS FERRY, OHIO

by James Wright

In the Shreve High football stadium,
I think of Polacks nursing long beers in Tiltonsville,
And gray faces of Negroes in the blast furnace at Benwood,
And the ruptured night watchman of Wheeling Steel,
Dreaming of heroes.

All the proud fathers are ashamed to go home.
Their women cluck like starved pullets,
Dying for love.

Therefore,
Their sons grow suicidally beautiful
At the beginning of October,
And gallop terribly against each other's bodies.

■ ■ ■

CLEARLY THROUGH MY TEARS

by Susan Love Fitts

Clearly through my tears I see
your fragility in the
strains of Chopin's piano,
something that must be listened
to with care
saying much with few notes.
I must turn everything off
or I could miss
what you're telling me.

Clearly through my tears I see
your pain on the face of a nameless child
walking the street
wondering,
wandering,
thoughts of herself
her unbeautiful self,
her body,
her intellect—is there any?

Clearly through my tears I see
you striving to cope in this world
not so easy for a tender one
hard to stand with the wind

blowing all around
disheveling your hair
making your eyes squint so you
can't see where you're going.

I see you now.

■ ■ ■

WHEN I WAS A KID IN NUEVA YORK

by Alvin Delgado

When I was a kid in Nueva York
    I was always afraid to sleep alone
    Eyes stretched behind nylon stockings
    Scared me more than Aunt Carlina's
    Beaded curtains, flickering candles
    African masks, petal baths and ghosts

    I remember, a night, burglars
    Smashed a window above my floor

    I cannot open my mouth

    Cars rush down the streets
    Steam whistles heated pipes
    A cat meows outside
    A toilet flushes two floors up
    Burglars quietly take and move
    In the darkness of apartments
    Shortness of breath I faint

    The next day I cannot sleep
    Waiting by my parents' room
    With a blanket and a boot
    "Go back to bed," my father says
    Days later we end up in Radio Shack

We buy a huge white horn
With long twisted wires
The magnets stuck at the bottom
Corners of windowpanes
My father flicks the switch
The alarm is on

Another burglar makes a pass
A silhouette presses on the glass
Then blends into the darkness
Under the covers urine reeks everywhere
As I lie frozen on a warm wet mattress

■ ■ ■

THE WORLD IS TOO MUCH WITH US

by William Wordsworth

The world is too much with us; late and soon,
Getting and spending, we lay waste our powers:
Little we see in Nature that is ours;
We have given our hearts away, a sordid boon!
This Sea that bares her bosom to the moon;
The winds that will be howling at all hours,
And are up-gathered now like sleeping flowers;
For this, for every thing, we are out of tune;
It moves us not. — Great God! I'd rather be
A Pagan suckled in a creed outworn;
So might I, standing on this pleasant lea,
Have glimpses that would make me less forlorn;
Have sight of Proteus rising from the sea;
Or hear old Triton blow his wreathèd horn.

■ ■ ■

Lopsided
LOVE

THE FOLLY OF BEING COMFORTED

by W. B. Yeats

One that is ever kind said yesterday:
'Your well-beloved's hair has threads of grey,
And little shadows come about her eyes;
Time can but make it easier to be wise
Though now it seem impossible, and so
All that you need is patience.'

Heart cries, 'No,

I have not a crumb of comfort, not a grain.
Time can but make her beauty over again:
Because of that great nobleness of hers
The fire that stirs about her, when she stirs,
Burns but more clearly. O she had not these ways
When all the wild summer was in her gaze.'

O heart! O heart! if she'd but turn her head,
You'd know the folly of being comforted.

■ ■ ■

HE BIDS HIS BELOVED BE AT PEACE

by W. B. Yeats

I hear the Shadowy Horses, their long manes a-shake,
Their hoofs heavy with tumult, their eyes glimmering white;
The North unfolds above them clinging, creeping night,
The East her hidden joy before the morning break,
The West weeps in pale dew and sighs passing away,
The South is pouring down roses of crimson fire:
O vanity of Sleep, Hope, Dream, endless Desire,
The Horses of Disaster plunge in the heavy clay:
Beloved, let your eyes half close, and your heart beat
Over my heart, and your hair fall over my breast,
Drowning love's lonely hour in deep twilight of rest,
And hiding their tossing manes and their tumultuous feet.

■ ■ ■

DISCORD IN CHILDHOOD

by D. H. Lawrence

Outside the house an ash-tree hung its terrible whips,
And at night when the wind rose, the lash of the tree
Shrieked and slashed the wind, as a ship's
Weird rigging in a storm shrieks hideously.

Within the house two voices arose, a slender lash
Whistling delirious rage, and the dreadful sound
Of a thick lash booming and bruising, until it had drowned
The other voice in a silence of blood, 'neath the noise
      of the ash.

■ ■ ■

ANECDOTE

by Dorothy Parker

So silent I when Love was by
      He yawned, and turned away;
But Sorrow clings to my apron-strings,
      I have so much to say.

■ ■ ■

AUTUMN VALENTINE

by Dorothy Parker

In May my heart was breaking—
    Oh, wide the wound, and deep!
And bitter it beat at waking,
    And sore it split in sleep.

And when it came November,
    I sought my heart, and sighed,
"Poor thing, do you remember?"
    "What heart was that?" it cried.

■ ■ ■

THE LOVE SONG OF J. ALFRED PRUFROCK

by T. S. Eliot

S'io credesse che mia risposta fosse
A persona che mai tornasse al mondo,
Questa fiamma staria senza piu scosse.
Ma perciocche giammai di questo fondo
Non torno vivo alcun, s'i'odo il vero,
Senza tema d'infamia ti rispondo.

Let us go then, you and I,
When the evening is spread out against the sky
Like a patient etherised upon a table;
Let us go, through certain half-deserted streets,
The muttering retreats
Of restless nights in one-night cheap hotels
And sawdust restaurants with oyster-shells:
Streets that follow like a tedious argument
Of insidious intent
To lead you to an overwhelming question . . .
Oh, do not ask, "What is it?"
Let us go and make our visit.

In the room the women come and go
Talking of Michelangelo.

The yellow fog that rubs its back upon the window-panes,
The yellow smoke that rubs its muzzle on the window-panes
Licked its tongue into the corners of the evening,
Lingered upon the pools that stand in drains,
Let fall upon its back the soot that falls from chimneys,
Slipped by the terrace, made a sudden leap,
And seeing that it was a soft October night,
Curled once about the house, and fell asleep.

And indeed there will be time
For the yellow smoke that slides along the street,
Rubbing its back upon the window-panes;
There will be time, there will be time
To prepare a face to meet the faces that you meet;
There will be time to murder and create,
And time for all the works and days of hands
That lift and drop a question on your plate;
Time for you and time for me,
And time yet for a hundred indecisions,
And for a hundred visions and revisions,
Before the taking of a toast and tea.

In the room the women come and go
Talking of Michelangelo.

And indeed there will be time
To wonder, "Do I dare?" and, "Do I dare?"
Time to turn back and descend the stair,
With a bald spot in the middle of my hair—
[They will say: "How his hair is growing thin!"]
My morning coat, my collar mounting firmly to the chin,
My necktie rich and modest, but asserted by a simple pin—
[They will say: "But how his arms and legs are thin!"]
Do I dare
Disturb the universe?
In a minute there is time
For decisions and revisions which a minute will reverse.

For I have known them all already, known them all:—
Have known the evenings, mornings, afternoons,
I have measured out my life with coffee spoons;
I know the voices dying with a dying fall
Beneath the music from a farther room.
    So how should I presume?

And I have known the eyes already, known them all—
The eyes that fix you in a formulated phrase,
And when I am formulated, sprawling on a pin,
When I am pinned and wriggling on the wall,
Then how should I begin
To spit out all the butt-ends of my days and ways?
    And how should I presume?

And I have known the arms already, known them all—
Arms that are braceleted and white and bare
[But in the lamplight, downed with light brown hair!]
It is perfume from a dress
That makes me so digress?
Arms that lie along a table, or wrap about a shawl.
        And should I then presume?
        And how should I begin?

———

Shall I say, I have gone at dusk through narrow streets
And watched the smoke that rises from the pipes
Of lonely men in shirt-sleeves, leaning out of windows? . . .

I should have been a pair of ragged claws
Scuttling across the floors of silent seas.

———

And the afternoon, the evening, sleeps so peacefully!
Smoothed by long fingers,
Asleep . . . tired . . . or it malingers,
Stretched on the floor, here beside you and me.
Should I, after tea and cakes and ices,
Have the strength to force the moment to its crisis?
But though I have wept and fasted, wept and prayed,
Though I have seen my head [grown slightly bald] brought
        in upon a platter,
I am no prophet—and here's no great matter;
I have seen the moment of my greatness flicker,

And I have seen the eternal Footman hold my coat,
    and snicker,
And in short, I was afraid.

And would it have been worth it, after all,
After the cups, the marmalade, the tea,
Among the porcelain, among some talk of you and me,
Would it have been worth while,
To have bitten off the matter with a smile,
To have squeezed the universe into a ball
To roll it toward some overwhelming question,
To say: "I am Lazarus, come from the dead,
Come back to tell you all, I shall tell you all"—
If one, settling a pillow by her head,
        Should say: "That is not what I meant at all.
        That is not it, at all."

And would it have been worth it, after all,
Would it have been worth while,
After the sunsets and the dooryards and the sprinkled streets,
After the novels, after the teacups, after the skirts that trail
    along the floor—
And this, and so much more?—
It is impossible to say just what I mean!
But as if a magic lantern threw the nerves in patterns on a
        screen:
Would it have been worth while
If one, settling a pillow or throwing off a shawl,
And turning toward the window, should say:

"That is not it at all,
    That is not what I meant, at all."

———

No! I am not Prince Hamlet, nor was meant to be;
Am an attendant lord, one that will do
To swell a progress, start a scene or two,
Advise the prince; no doubt, an easy tool,
Deferential, glad to be of use,
Politic, cautious, and meticulous;
Full of high sentence, but a bit obtuse;
At times, indeed, almost ridiculous—
Almost, at times, the Fool.

I grow old . . . I grow old . . .
I shall wear the bottoms of my trousers rolled.

Shall I part my hair behind? Do I dare to eat a peach?
I shall wear white flannel trousers, and walk upon the beach.
I have heard the mermaids singing, each to each.

I do not think that they will sing to me.

I have seen them riding seaward on the waves
Combing the white hair of the waves blown back
When the wind blows the water white and black.

We have lingered in the chambers of the sea
By sea-girls wreathed with seaweed red and brown
Till human voices wake us, and we drown.

■ ■ ■

From A MIDSUMMER NIGHT'S DREAM

by William Shakespeare

Lovers and madmen have such seething brains,
Such shaping fantasies, that apprehend
More than cool reason ever comprehends.
The lunatic, the lover, and the poet
Are of imagination all compact.
One sees more devils than vast hell can hold:
That is the madman. The lover, all as frantic,
Sees Helen's beauty in a brow of Egypt.
The poet's eye, in a fine frenzy rolling,
Doth glance from heaven to earth, from earth to heaven,
And as imagination bodies forth
The forms of things unknown, the poet's pen
Turns them to shapes and gives to airy nothing
A local habitation and a name.
Such tricks hath strong imagination
That, if it would but apprehend some joy,
It comprehends some bringer of that joy.
Or in the night, imagining some fear,
How easy is a bush supposed a bear!

■ ■ ■

WASTED

by June Jordan

You should slice the lying tongue of your love
into a billion bits of bile you swallow
one bilious element at a time
while
scalding water trembles drop
by drop between
(you hope)
between your eyes because
you said you loved me
and you lied
you lied

All you wanted was to rid me of my pride
to ruin me for tenderness
you lied
to thrust me monstrous from the hurt
you fabricated claiming
all the opposites of pain
while maiming
me
the victim of your whimsical disdain

And I still love you like the river
in the rain
in vain
you lied
in vain.

■ ■ ■

ONE ART

by Elizabeth Bishop

The art of losing isn't hard to master;
so many things seem filled with the intent
to be lost that their loss is no disaster.

Lose something every day. Accept the fluster
of lost door keys, the hour badly spent.
The art of losing isn't hard to master.

Then practice losing farther, losing faster:
places, and names, and where it was you meant
to travel. None of these will bring disaster.

I lost my mother's watch. And look! my last, or
next-to-last, of three loved houses went.
The art of losing isn't hard to master.

I lost two cities, lovely ones. And, vaster,
some realms I owned, two rivers, a continent.
I miss them, but it wasn't a disaster.

—Even losing you (the joking voice, a gesture
I love) I shan't have lied. It's evident
the art of losing's not too hard to master
though it may look like (*Write* it!) like disaster.

■ ■ ■

MELBA STREET
(For Johnny)

by Deena November

Tonight the lights went out
and I'm still his in the kitchen mess,
my boyfriend runs down to the basement to ignore me and
     please himself,
while I wait for him to come back with some sort of
     craziness in his hands,
I hear a clink clink of tin cans from the stairs
that jilt and confuse me

my boyfriend returning moments later,
Silent, sniffling and holding paint cans.

In this house of fools and books,
where toilets don't flush,
and heated rooms turn to bitter aggravation,
here where my boyfriend's manic depressive
brush strokes the fake wood paneled walls
house where long cobblestoned streets of rejection halt,
                          where plastic
wood
and my pants turn white,
                house where people overreact,
and sleep close together,

I need the mass of my boyfriend's lips,
need to see how the white paint looked on
the wood panels of his head
                      not to swivel
into ignorance.

■■■

ALWAYS SECONDARY

by Deena November

i'll always be the dish you're stuck with when
the waitress returns from the kitchen to tell
you they're out of steak but hey, you can have me,
the wilted vegetable of last week's side special.

for five years i waitressed so i know the trick but
i won't push wilted vegetables upon a carnivore. i know
men who would eat vegetables for a main course. so go to
another restaurant and get the steak and leave that waitress
a 33% tip

because i'm an old empty alphabet soup can to flick ashes
into while the ashtray is temporarily
taken away for emptying.

i'm the plane an hour after you've missed your first flight
that one-way ticket home. i'm the one with connecting
flights that puts you on standby.

call me up after all you know sleep
and insomnia guides you to me
by default

■■■

WHEN WE TWO PARTED

by Lord Byron

When we two parted
In silence and tears,
Half broken-hearted
To sever for years,
Pale grew thy cheek and cold,
Colder thy kiss;
Truly that hour foretold
Sorrow to this.

The dew of the morning
Sunk chill on my brow—
It felt like the warning
Of what I feel now.
Thy vows are all broken,
And light is thy fame;
I hear thy name spoken,
And share in its shame.

They name thee before me,
A knell to mine ear;
A shudder comes o'er me—
Why wert thou so dear?
They know not I knew thee,
Who knew thee too well:—
Long, long shall I rue thee,
Too deeply to tell.

In secret we meet—
In silence I grieve,
That thy heart could forget,
Thy spirit deceive.
If I should meet thee
After long years,
How should I greet thee?—
With silence and tears.

■ ■ ■

HOW HEAVY THE DAYS . . .

by Hermann Hesse
Translated by James Wright

How heavy the days are.
There's not a fire to warm me,
Not a sun to laugh with me,
Everything bare,
Everything cold and merciless,
And even the beloved, clear
Stars look desolately down,
Since I learned in my heart that
Love can die.

■ ■ ■

FALL ON ME

by Kate Schmitt

Absolute cold; absence of things.
A hundred blankets, a hundred years old,
pieces of an unsewn quilt,
patches of light
through the curtains.

All night your hand is on my shoulder,
branding it in designs of sleep.
I stared at your face, the wall,
heard engines and wheels on wet pavement.

All my life I have been waiting.
Like the comet this spring, I waited
to burn, to follow myself
with a hot trail of dust and light,
be utterly consumed.

And now this space, this room.
I realize there are no rules anymore.
The windows and walls seem flimsy,
as if the world might fall on me
the way you do.

■ ■ ■

THE TAXI

by Amy Lowell

When I go away from you
The world beats dead
Like a slackened drum.
I call out for you against the jutted stars
And shout into the ridges of the wind.
Streets coming fast,
One after the other,
Wedge you away from me,
And the lamps of the city prick my eyes
So that I can no longer see your face.
Why should I leave you,
To wound myself upon the sharp edges of the night?

■ ■ ■

"YOU DON'T HAVE 'BAD' DAYS AND 'GOOD' DAYS"

by Rumi

Translated by Coleman Barks

You don't have "bad" days and "good" days.
You don't sometimes feel brilliant and sometimes dumb.
There's no studying, no scholarly thinking having to do
    with love,
but there is a great deal of plotting, and secret touching,
and nights you can't remember at all.

■ ■ ■

"WHEN I AM WITH YOU, WE STAY UP ALL NIGHT"

by Rumi

Translated by Coleman Barks

When I am with you, we stay up all night.
When you're not here, I can't go to sleep.

Praise God for these two insomnias!
And the difference between them.

■ ■ ■

Rapid
TUMBLE

NO MOMENT PAST THIS ONE

by Stephen Dobyns

Yes, it seems like something out there.
Is it like a blanket? No, not like a blanket.
Is it like darkness? No, not like darkness.
But it doesn't act like something inside.
You ask how I know this? Because it seems
to be waiting. And it seems to have both
hunger and humor. And it seems both
patient and eager, both heavy and weightless.
And it is huge. And it grows immense.
How can it not be like darkness when
it eats the light? How can it not be like
a blanket when it seems all-enveloping?
How can it be a place to tumble into
yet be so tireless, so nimble? If I could
solve such riddles, then perhaps, perhaps,
but when it comes it ties me in soft ropes,
and it takes each drop of blood from me
and yet I continue to live, although there
seems no moment beyond this one and
this one and the days continue to pass by.
You see, it must come from the outside,
like a hunter just out of sight, because
if the beast lived within me, then how
could I live, how could it be withstood?

■■■

THE YEAR I FOUND

by Dieter Weslowski

my dead self in
the flowerbed, grey
as a marbleized salamander
beneath a bleed of
acorn roots, I placed
the devil mask from Cuernavaca
over the fireplace, counter
spell so to speak.
Then came the kicker—my wife
sickling down the tiger lilies
as I drove up the driveway
after a bad day at the Butlers'.

■■■

BROTHERHOOD

by Yehoshua November

The first boy to fall in
love with my then future wife
was a second-grader
with wild curly hair
and sharp eyes,
the class clown,
Maurice,

who accidentally signed
an anonymous love letter
he sent her in the mail,

who, in the shadows
of the school coatroom
uncloaked his sex
and held it before her eyes
like a rare, tropical fish
that would surely
die if left
too long in the open air.

Maurice,

I am told that

a few years later,
they put you in an institution.

And I imagine that
as you watched your father and mother's car
fade behind the sun
and a row of trees,
and turned your face
back to the asylum doors,

hundreds of miles away,
a heaviness found my heart.

■ ■ ■

DREAM SONG 22: "OF 1826"

by John Berryman

I am the little man who smokes & smokes.
I am the girl who does know better but.
I am the king of the pool.
I am so wise I had my mouth sewn shut.
I am a government official & a goddamned fool.
I am a lady who takes jokes.

I am the enemy of the mind.
I am the auto salesman and lóve you.
I am a teenage cancer, with a plan.
I am the blackt-out man.
I am the woman powerful as a zoo.
I am two eyes screwed to my set, whose blind—

It is the Fourth of July.
Collect: while the dying man,
forgone by you creator, who forgives,
is gasping 'Thomas Jefferson still lives'
in vain, in vain, in vain.
I am Henry Pussy-cat! My whiskers fly.

■ ■ ■

SKUNK HOUR
[For Elizabeth Bishop]

by Robert Lowell

Nautilus Island's hermit
heiress still lives through winter in her Spartan cottage;
her sheep still graze above the sea.
Her son's a bishop. Her farmer
is first selectman in our village;
she's in her dotage.

Thirsting for
the hierarchic privacy
of Queen Victoria's century,
she buys up all
the eyesores facing her shore,
and lets them fall.

The season's ill—
we've lost our summer millionaire,
who seemed to leap from an L. L. Bean
catalogue. His nine-knot yawl
was auctioned off to lobstermen.
A red fox stain covers Blue Hill.

And now our fairy
decorator brightens his shop for fall;
his fishnet's filled with orange cork,
orange, his cobbler's bench and awl;

there is no money in his work,
he'd rather marry.

One dark night,
my Tudor Ford climbed the hill's skull;
I watched for love-cars. Lights turned down,
they lay together, hull to hull,
where the graveyard shelves on the town. . . .
My mind's not right.

A car radio bleats,
"Love, O careless Love. . . ." I hear
my ill-spirit sob in each blood cell,
as if my hand were at its throat. . . .
I myself am hell;
nobody's here—

only skunks, that search
in the moonlight for a bite to eat.
They march on their soles up Main Street:
white stripes, moonstruck eyes' red fire
under the chalk-dry and spar spire
of the Trinitarian Church.

I stand on top
of our back steps and breathe the rich air—
a mother skunk with her column of kittens swills the
        garbage pail.
She jabs her wedge-head in a cup
of sour cream, drops her ostrich tail,
and will not scare.

■■■

THINGS

by Fleur Adcock

There are worse things than having behaved foolishly in
     public.
There are worse things than these miniature betrayals,
committed or endured or suspected; there are worse things
than not being able to sleep for thinking about them.
It is 5 a.m. All the worse things come stalking in
and stand icily about the bed looking worse and worse
                              and worse.

■ ■ ■

THE BELLS

by Edgar Allan Poe

I.

Hear the sledges with the bells—
　　　　Silver bells!
What a world of merriment their melody foretells!

　　How they tinkle, tinkle, tinkle,
　　　　In the icy air of night!
　　While the stars that oversprinkle
　　All the heavens, seem to twinkle
　　　　With a crystalline delight;
　　　　Keeping time, time, time
　　　　In a sort of Runic rhyme,
To the tintinnabulation that so musically wells
　From the bells, bells, bells, bells,
　　　　Bells, bells, bells—
　From the jingling and the tinkling of the bells.

II.

　　Hear the mellow wedding bells
　　　　Golden bells!
What a world of happiness their harmony foretells!
　　Through the balmy air of night
　　How they ring out their delight!—
　　　　From the molten-golden notes.
　　　　And all in tune,

What a liquid ditty floats
To the turtle-dove that listens, while she gloats
On the moon!
Oh, from out the sounding cells,
What a gush of euphony voluminously wells!
How it swells!
How it dwells
On the Future!—how it tells
Of the rapture that impels
To the swinging and the ringing
Of the bells, bells, bells—
Of the bells, bells, bells, bells,
Bells, bells, bells—
To the rhyming and the chiming of the bells!

III.

Hear the loud alarum bells—
Brazen bells!
What a tale of terror, now their turbulency tells!
In the startled ear of night
How they scream out their affright!
Too much horrified to speak,
They can only shriek, shriek,
Out of tune,
In a clamorous appealing to the mercy of the fire,
In a mad expostulation with the deaf and frantic fire,
Leaping higher, higher, higher,
With a desperate desire,
And a resolute endeavor

Now—now to sit, or never,
By the side of the pale-faced moon.
Oh, the bells, bells, bells!
What a tale their terror tells
Of Despair!
How they clang, and clash, and roar!
What a horror they outpour
On the bosom of the palpitating air!
Yet the ear, it fully knows,
By the twanging,
And the clanging,
How the danger ebbs and flows;
Yet the ear distinctly tells,
In the jangling,
And the wrangling,
How the danger sinks and swells,
By the sinking or the swelling in the anger of the bells—
Of the bells—
Of the bells, bells, bells, bells,
Bells, bells, bells—
In the clamor and the clangor of the bells!

IV.

Hear the tolling of the bells—
Iron bells!
What a world of solemn thought their monody compels!
In the silence of the night,
How we shiver with affright
At the melancholy menace of their tone!

For every sound that floats
From the rust within their throats
    Is a groan.
And the people—ah, the people—
They that dwell up in the steeple,
    All alone,
And who, tolling, tolling, tolling,
    In that muffled monotone,
Feel a glory in so rolling
    On the human heart a stone—
They are neither man nor woman—
They are neither brute nor human—
    They are Ghouls:—
And their king it is who tolls:—
And he rolls, rolls, rolls,
                Rolls
    A pæan from the bells!
And his merry bosom swells
    With the pæan of the bells!
And he dances, and he yells;
Keeping time, time, time,
In a sort of Runic rhyme,
    To the pæan of the bells:—
Of the bells:
Keeping time, time, time,
In a sort of Runic rhyme,
    To the throbbing of the bells—
Of the bells, bells, bells—
    To the sobbing of the bells:—

Keeping time, time, time,
  As he knells, knells, knells,
In a happy Runic rhyme,
  To the rolling of the bells—
Of the bells, bells, bells:—
  To the tolling of the bells—
Of the bells, bells, bells, bells,
  Bells, bells, bells—
To the moaning and the groaning of the bells.

■ ■ ■

HYSTERIA

by T. S. Eliot

As she laughed I was aware of becoming involved in her laughter and being part of it, until her teeth were only accidental stars with a talent for squad-drill. I was drawn in by short gasps, inhaled at each momentary recovery, lost finally in the dark caverns of her throat, bruised by the ripple of unseen muscles. An elderly waiter with trembling hands was hurriedly spreading a pink and white checked cloth over the rusty green iron table, saying: "If the lady and gentleman wish to take their tea in the garden, if the lady and gentleman wish to take their tea in the garden . . ." I decided that if the shaking of her breasts could be stopped, some of the fragments of the afternoon might be collected, and I concentrated my attention with careful subtlety to this end.

■ ■ ■

LADY LAZARUS

by Sylvia Plath

I have done it again.
One year in every ten
I manage it——

A sort of walking miracle, my skin
Bright as a Nazi lampshade,
My right foot

A paperweight,
My face a featureless, fine
Jew linen.

Peel off the napkin
O my enemy.
Do I terrify?——

The nose, the eye pits, the full set of teeth?
The sour breath
Will vanish in a day.

Soon, soon the flesh
The grave cave ate will be
At home on me

And I a smiling woman.
I am only thirty.
And like a cat I have nine times to die.

This is Number Three.
What a trash
To annihilate each decade.

What a million filaments.
The peanut-crunching crowd
Shoves in to see

Them unwrap me hand and foot—
The big strip tease.
Gentlemen, ladies,

These are my hands,
My knees.
I may be skin and bone,

Nevertheless, I am the same, identical woman.
The first time it happened I was ten.
It was an accident.

The second time I meant
to last it out and not come back at all.
I rocked shut

As a seashell.
They had to call and call
And pick the worms off me like sticky pearls.

Dying
Is an art, like everything else.
I do it exceptionally well.

I do it so it feels like hell.
I do it so it feels real.
I guess you could say I've a call.

It's easy enough to do it in a cell.
It's easy enough to do it and stay put.
It's the theatrical

Comeback in broad day
To the same place, the same face, the same brute
Amused shout:

"A miracle!"
That knocks me out.
There is a charge

For the eyeing of my scars, there is a charge
For the hearing of my heart—
It really goes.

And there is a charge, a very large charge,
For a word or a touch
Or a bit of blood

Or a piece of my hair or my clothes.
So, so, Herr Doktor.
So, Herr Enemy.

I am your opus,
I am your valuable,
The pure gold baby

That melts to a shriek.
I turn and burn.
Do not think I underestimate your great concern.

Ash, ash—
You poke and stir.
Flesh, bone, there is nothing there—

A cake of soap.
A wedding ring,
A gold filling.

Herr God, Herr Lucifer,
Beware
Beware.

Out of the ash
I rise with my red hair
And I eat men like air.

■ ■ ■

HAVING IT OUT WITH MELANCHOLY

by Jane Kenyon

If many remedies are prescribed for an illness,
you may be certain that the illness has no cure.

—A. P. Chekhov
The Cherry Orchard

1 FROM THE NURSERY

When I was born, you waited
behind a pile of linen in the nursery,
and when we were alone, you lay down
on top of me, pressing
the bile of desolation into every pore.

And from that day on
everything under the sun and moon
made me sad—even the yellow
wooden beads that slid and spun
along a spindle on my crib.

You taught me to exist without gratitude.
You ruined my manners toward God:
"We're here simply to wait for death;
the pleasures of earth are overrated."

I only appeared to belong to my mother,
to live among blocks and cotton undershirts
with snaps; among red tin lunch boxes

and report cards in ugly brown slipcases.
I was already yours—the anti-urge,
the mutilator of souls.

2 BOTTLES

Elavil, Ludiomil, Doxepin,
Norpramin, Prozac, Lithium, Xanax,
Wellbutrin, Parnate, Nardil, Zoloft.
The coated ones smell sweet or have
no smell; the powdery ones smell
like the chemistry lab at school
that made me hold my breath.

3 SUGGESTION FROM A FRIEND

You wouldn't be so depressed
if you really believed in God.

4 OFTEN

Often I go to bed as soon after dinner
as seems adult
(I mean I try to wait for dark)
in order to push away
from the massive pain in sleep's
frail wicker coracle.

5 ONCE THERE WAS LIGHT

Once, in my early thirties, I saw
that I was a speck of light in the great
river of light that undulates through time.

I was floating with the whole
human family. We were all colors — those
who are living now, those who have died,
those who are not yet born. For a few

moments I floated, completely calm,
and I no longer hated having to exist.

Like a crow who smells hot blood
you came flying to pull me out
of the glowing stream.
"I'll hold you up. I never let my dear
ones drown!" After that, I wept for days.

6 IN AND OUT

The dog searches until he finds me
upstairs, lies down with a clatter
of elbows, puts his head on my foot.

Sometimes the sound of his breathing
saves my life — in and out, in
and out; a pause, a long sigh. . . .

7 PARDON

A piece of burned meat
wears my clothes, speaks
in my voice, dispatches obligations
haltingly, or not at all.
It is tired of trying
to be stouthearted, tired
beyond measure.

We move on to the monoamine
oxidase inhibitors. Day and night
I feel as if I had drunk six cups
of coffee, but the pain stops
abruptly. With the wonder
and bitterness of someone pardoned
for a crime she did not commit
I come back to marriage and friends,
to pink-fringed hollyhocks; come back
to my desk, books, and chair.

8 CREDO

Pharmaceutical wonders are at work
but I believe only in this moment
of well-being. Unholy ghost,
you are certain to come again.

Coarse, mean, you'll put your feet
on the coffee table, lean back,
and turn me into someone who can't

take the trouble to speak; someone
who can't sleep, or who does nothing
but sleep; can't read, or call
for an appointment for help.

There is nothing I can do
against your coming.
When I awake, I am still with thee.

9 WOOD THRUSH

High on Nardil and June light
I wake at four,
waiting greedily for the first
notes of the wood thrush. Easeful air
presses through the screen
with the wild, complex song
of the bird, and I am overcome

by ordinary contentment.
What hurt me so terribly
all my life until this moment?
How I love the small, swiftly
beating heart of the bird
singing in the great maples;
its bright, unequivocal eye.

■ ■ ■

PRELUDE TO THE FALL

by Kate Schmitt

The light is different here.
It isn't mine
except some dark morning twilights

and even then I can't get out of bed.

I felt it coming on for months,
a moss growing up my ankles,
a slowing in the gristle of my joints.

Gravity is strong here.
On patches of grass and pine needles
I have to drag myself by my arms
toward the car

I got so tired of walking.
Gravity is patched with grass and pine needles.
Then the dreams about sweating,
it was all so hard. In the dreams I was trying
to make my nails grow.
I was tired. I'd never been so tired.

Eighty hours in bed.

Of the bed, I remember a kindness,
a sort of sweet distance from the window.
And my mother, I think she was sad—
her electric dryness leaning in my
door jamb. I smiled crack-lipped at her.

Eighty hours.
I couldn't get up. I don't remember getting up.

■ ■ ■

FALLEN

by Kate Schmitt

They walk into us
like rooms
so that every night I gasp
for breath in a sea
of tossed sheets.
The moon is full.
I know this
the way you know
someone has been in your house
even before you walk through the door.

Light spills in two-hour rounds
onto our faces at night.
Outside is illuminated a sickly yellow.
We have cut our hair, our legs,
small tears in the fabric of the body.
We have been defeated by slippers,

our courage lost in tiny paper cups
filled with our unused happiness.

■ ■ ■

THE WAKING

by Theodore Roethke

I wake to sleep, and take my waking slow.
I feel my fate in what I cannot fear.
I learn by going where I have to go.

We think by feeling. What is there to know?
I hear my being dance from ear to ear.
I wake to sleep, and take my waking slow.

Of those so close beside me, which are you?
God bless the Ground! I shall walk softly there,
And learn by going where I have to go.

Light takes the Tree; but who can tell us how?
The lowly worm climbs up a winding stair;
I wake to sleep, and take my waking slow.

Great Nature has another thing to do
To you and me; so take the lively air,
And, lovely, learn by going where to go.

This shaking keeps me steady. I should know.
What falls away is always. And is near.
I wake to sleep, and take my waking slow.
I learn by going where I have to go.

■ ■ ■

JEALOUSY

by Elaine Restifo

I've watched a young woman fondling three strands
     of her own hair
In the back seat of a Maserati. She said, "I am so young
And beautiful I won't exert myself precipitously.
Watch my blue eyes, the way I toss my hair,
The boredom in my perfect shoulder."

When I was young, back there in an old truck without tires,
Playing house with baby sister, we had our own
     Christmas tree
In February. There were shreds of tinsel hanging on it still.
We balanced small pieces of colored glass carefully
On its branches. It was cold, Foster Mother drunk.
Her broken brother chased us through the attic one day,
Lower denture hanging out, smelly blanket on his shoulders.
Dad hadn't beaten me up yet. I was six.

■ ■ ■

BABBLE

by César Vallejo

Translated by John Knoepfle

Meek house with no style, framed
with a single knock and a single piece
of rainbow wax. And in the house
she destroys and she cleans; says at times:
"The asylum is nice. Where? Here!"
Other times she breaks down and cries.

■ ■ ■

I TOLD THEM I SHOULD BE HERE

by Kate Schmitt

Protected. I was bent
like a piece of wire, I said.

There are two chairs. Vinyl. A desk.
A locked cabinet and a scale.
A paperclip.

There is a reason for all of this.
But not for me.

I have markings like a beetle,
thin white lines
that are covered in sleeves, bruises
shiny as fish scales.
They are looking at me
and the metal doors look cold and smooth.
I would like to press my cheek
against them. The light is copper,
a tarnished kettle.

I measure distances,
Small victories against the darkness.
I remember.

I couldn't know what would come next.
But I told them, the sweetness
Of each powdery white dot sliding down.

■ ■ ■

WANTING TO DIE

by Anne Sexton

Since you ask, most days I cannot remember.
I walk in my clothing, unmarked by that voyage.
Then the almost unnameable lust returns.

Even then I have nothing against life.
I know well the grass blades you mention,
the furniture you have placed under the sun.

But suicides have a special language.
Like carpenters they want to know *which tools.*
They never ask *why build.*

Twice I have so simply declared myself,
have possessed the enemy, eaten the enemy,
have taken on his craft, his magic.

In this way, heavy and thoughtful,
warmer than oil or water,
I have rested, drooling at the mouth-hole.

I did not think of my body at needle point.
Even the cornea and the leftover urine were gone.
Suicides have already betrayed the body.

Still-born, they don't always die,
but dazzled, they can't forget a drug so sweet
that even children would look on and smile.

To thrust all that life under your tongue!—
that, all by itself, becomes a passion.
Death's a sad bone; bruised, you'd say,

and yet she waits for me, year after year,
to so delicately undo an old wound,
to empty my breath from its bad prison.

Balanced there, suicides sometimes meet,
raging at the fruit, a pumped-up moon,
leaving the bread they mistook for a kiss,

leaving the page of the book carelessly open,
something unsaid, the phone off the hook
and the love, whatever it was, an infection.

■ ■ ■

MAD SONG

by William Blake

The wild winds weep,
    And the night is a-cold;
Come hither, Sleep,
    And my griefs enfold.
But lo! the morning peeps
    Over the eastern steeps,
And the rustling birds of dawn
The earth do scorn.

Lo! to the vault
    Of paved heaven,
With sorrow fraught
    My notes are driven;
They strike the ear of night,
    Make weep the eyes of day;
They make mad the roaring winds,
And with tempests play.

Like a fiend in a cloud
    With howling woe,
After night I do crowd,
    And with night will go;
I turn my back to the east,
    From whence comforts have increased;
For light doth seize my brain
With frantic pain.

■ ■ ■

"THE FIRST DAY'S NIGHT HAD COME"

by Emily Dickinson

The first Day's Night had come—
And grateful that a thing
So terrible—had been endured—
I told my Soul to sing—

She said her Strings were snapt—
Her Bow—to Atoms blown—
And so to mend her—gave me work
Until another Morn—

And then—a Day as huge
As Yesterdays in pairs,
Unrolled its horror in my face—
Until it blocked my eyes—

My Brain—begun to laugh—
I mumbled—like a fool—
And tho' 'tis Years ago—that Day—
My Brain keeps giggling—still.

And Something's odd—within—
That person that I was—
And this One—do not feel the same—
Could it be Madness—this?

■ ■ ■

LINES WRITTEN DURING A PERIOD OF INSANITY (1774)

by William Cowper

Hatred and vengeance, my eternal portion,
Scarce can endure delay of execution,
Wait, with impatient readiness, to seize my
                Soul in a moment.

Damn'd below Judas: more abhorr'd than he was,
Who for a few pence sold his holy Master.
Twice betrayed Jesus me, the last delinquent,
                Deems the profanest.

Man disavows, and Deity disowns me:
Hell might afford my miseries a shelter;
Therefore hell keeps her ever hungry mouths all
                Bolted against me.

Hard lot! encompass'd with a thousand dangers;
Weary, faint, trembling with a thousand terrors;
I'm called, if vanquish'd, to receive a sentence
                Worse than Abiram's.

Him the vindictive rod of angry justice
Sent quick and howling to the centre headlong;
I, fed with judgment, in a fleshly tomb, am
                Buried above ground.

■■■

NATIONAL DEPRESSION AWARENESS WEEK

by Mary Ruefle

The Scotch mist is a shroud
the wee rabbits are galumphing
and the crag speaks to the lonely glen.

The French cross-slice long baguettes
remove the soft white insides
and wear the crusts upon their wrists.

We planted all the tulips upside down!
Fortunately for us they were unimported.

Christ is way too big for that donkey.
But his hand has been up so long!

A stack of mattresses was piled on the sidewalk,
a reminder the next generation would spring
from their satiny tops and feel the pea-sized future.

I covered a gum wrapper with my foot,
destroying all evidence someone was here before me.

The last miserable months of my disastrous life
were spent trying to get a word in edgewise.

■■■

ANONYMOUS

by Susan Love Fitts

To the Department of Motor Vehicles
    I am my car tag number.

To the Department of Transportation
    I am my driver's license number.

To my insurance company
    I am both of the above.

To the Internet
    I am a screen name and a password,
    neither of which is My Name.

To the clerk at the grocery store and
everywhere else I shop,
    I am the number on my Visa card.

To the doctor's office
    I'm a patient number.

To the country club,
    I am a membership number.

To the taxing authorities in my country,
>I am an account number;
>>and/or
>the person living on this lot number,
>that block number,
>and some subdivision number.

To the IRS,
the Social Security Administration,
my local bank,
and everyone else on the planet
>I am a Social Security number.

If someone wants to call me,
they can't simply pick up the phone and say
My Name.
Unless, of course, they possess of one of those
fancy voice activated devices; which,
unable to deal with my humanity,
quickly depersonalizes me into a series of digits.

Most necessary that we use abstractions
to live in a concrete world.

Nobody knows My Name anymore.
Except,
there was that little pub in Boston.

I'll have the special brew of the day, please:

>*Anonymous Ale!*

■ ■ ■

"THERE IS A LIGHT SEED GRAIN INSIDE"

by Rumi

Translated by Coleman Barks

There is a light seed grain inside.
You fill it with yourself, or it dies.

I'm caught in this curling energy! Your hair!
Whoever's calm and sensible is insane!

■ ■ ■

WISH
You
Were
HERE:

The
RETURN

SO, WE'LL GO NO MORE A ROVING

by Lord Byron

So, we'll go no more a roving
        So late into the night,
Though the heart be still as loving,
        And the moon be still as bright.

For the sword outwears its sheath,
        And the soul wears out the breast,
And the heart must pause to breathe,
        And love itself have rest.

Though the night was made for loving,
        And the day returns too soon,
Yet we'll go no more a-roving
        By the light of the moon.

■ ■ ■

POEMS OF DELIGHT

by Liz Rosenberg

1.

My friend Henry signs his note by accident
Henry
Henry
and writes, As a friend
I want to hold you.
Henry   Henry   we all want to be held.

2.

Coming home from summer school this year
I carried back: chocolate chip cookies;
          a wind-up grasshopper;
two birds; a feather; a rock; a shell
and a small brass turtle to wear or hold.
What have I given?

3.

Now I take three white pills
each day instead of two.
One comes in the middle, alone.
I can pretend I am having high tea
when I swallow it with water. Something
is beginning to lift.

4.

The first September breeze fluttered
across the tops
of the withered grass
and fall came tumbling in as
if someone had thrown
open a door.

5.

Last week I considered slitting my throat.
Imagined it painless and bloodless,
then pictured the mess.
Today I pick up the dirty dishes,
grumbling, and glad
to be grumbling.

6.

My husband reads from *Peter Pan* aloud:
a great book. I could never write
such a book. I put my jealousy away,
and climb under my son's covers
beside him, to listen.
Words, words, sing us to sleep.

7.

At the downtown audio-visual library
they have found two new James Herriott tapes.
And I can borrow both.
This means I have five—one more

than I'm allowed, and we all know it.
The librarian smiles and waves as I run out the door.

8.

My mother's old gold watch,
newly repaired, circles
my wrist, slides loosely around
and around; and on the other wrist
a bracelet with tiny green glass beads
throws rainbows over the steering wheel!

9.

I can go to a movie tonight.
I can eat Raisinets,
and maybe the chocolate won't make me crazy,
and if I am lucky
I'll find something to laugh about in the movie,
or something good to cry over.

10.

I've been so depressed that all my clothing fits, and I look
        good in everything.
Black especially.
Maybe my mother will see me while I'm still thin,
but not too bleak. You look good, she'll tell me,
        and I'll say, Ma, I feel good.

■ ■ ■

RAISING MY HAND

by Antler

One of the first things we learn in school is
       if we know the answer to a question
We must raise our hand and be called on
       before we can speak.
How strange it seemed to me then,
       raising my hand to be called on,
How at first I just blurted out,
       but that was not permitted.

How often I knew the answer
And the teacher (knowing I knew)
Called on others I knew (and she knew)
       had it wrong!
How I'd stretch my arm
       as if it would break free
       and shoot through the roof
       like a rocket!
How I'd wave and groan and sigh,
Even hold up my aching arm
       with my other hand
Begging to be called on,
Please, *me*, I know the answer!
Almost leaping from my seat
       hoping to hear my name.

Twenty-nine now, alone in the wilds,
Seated on some rocky outcrop
　　　　under all the stars,
I find myself raising my hand
　　　　as I did in first grade
Mimicking the excitement
　　　　and expectancy felt then.
No one calls on me
　　　　but the wind.

■ ■ ■

nobody but you

by Charles Bukowski

nobody can save you but
yourself.
you will be put again and again
into nearly impossible
situations.
they will attempt again and again
through subterfuge, guise and
force
to make you submit, quit and/or die quietly
inside.

nobody can save you but
yourself
and it will be easy enough to fail
so very easily
but don't, don't, don't.
just watch them.
listen to them.
do you want to be like *that*?
a faceless, mindless, heartless
being?
do you want to experience
death before death?

nobody can save you but
yourself

and you're worth saving.
it's a war not easily won
but if anything is worth winning then
this is it.

think about it.
think about saving your self.
your spiritual self.
your gut self.
your singing magical self and
your beautiful self.
save it.
don't join the dead-in-spirit.

maintain your self
with humor and grace
and finally
if necessary
wager your life as you struggle,
damn the odds, damn
the price.

only you can save your
self.

do it! do it!

then you'll know exactly what
I am talking about.

■ ■ ■

WINDOW BOX

by Thomas Scott Fisken

I strike the keys,
typing the poetry
unreeling
on the screen
outside my window
under the pool blue sky.

The thatched hair toddler
strains on the taut leash
of his mother's hand.
His arced spine
billows like a sail.
She tugs him
from the curb
of the vacant street.

I often go to the window,
drawn to a world called normal,
from the vantage
of a mind called abnormal.

Strolling home from shul,
Our neighbor
stumbles
on a crack in the concrete.
His shiny broad-band black hat

conceals his face,
as his eyes study
the coarse grass
sprouting
from the broken pavement.

The gray sky hunches.
Velvet-red geraniums shiver
in the anxious September air.

A ponytailed girl
(maybe twelve)
in ruby sandals and a coral tee
twirls a feathered violet scarf
draped from her shoulders—
a star from the black-and-white era
colorized on my TV.

Last night's rain
slicks the macadam.

Across the street
a baby screams
again and again
and again.
His howls are drowned
by the whine of a leaf blower.
Flattening my nose
to the mesh of the screen,
I can just see

the black hose
cycling the leather leaves
ripped from the trees
by an impatient wind.
Leaves
with no chance
to blaze
scarlet or orange or gold.

Mom shuts the window.
My eardrums hum
with the after-tremors.
The baby is silent.

The clouds scud by,
rimmed by occluded rays
casting flickering shadows.

An Asian man
in sky blue Bermudas
meanders on his bicycle.
His silver hair riffles.
His oxblood briefcase
hangs from the handlebars.

Tentative sunlight
gilds the boxed hedges.

The stout mailman
with an ash crewcut
stops to chat

with the woman in olive shorts
who lives diagonally
across the way.

Sudden rain needles
pierce the sun-shafts.

Zookeepers
in neon
tangerine shirts and gloves
toss hefty bags
into the grinding hinged maw
of the voracious beast.

Stuck behind,
the driver of a charcoal SUV
glances away
bored,
as our flung rubber cans
bounce
from the curb.

The shards of rain vanish.
The tentative sun
gilds the boxed hedges.

The blue serene
draws me to my doorway.
Stepping outside
I blink in the sun.

A snow-winged butterfly
weaves
through the black iron railing
by the brick stairs.
Swerving,
it zigs
to the knobbed trunk of the maple
across the street,
then zags
to the ivy-smothered hedge
next door.

The rusted porch swing
groans on its runners,
while I
rock

watching

■■■

BACK

by Jane Kenyon

We try a new drug, a new combination
of drugs, and suddenly
I fall into my life again

like a vole picked up by a storm
then dropped three valleys
and two mountains away from home.

I can find my way back. I know
I will recognize the store
where I used to buy milk and gas.

I remember the house and barn,
the rake, the blue cups and plates,
the Russian novels I loved so much,

and the black silk nightgown
that he once thrust
into the toe of my Christmas stocking.

■ ■ ■

THE JOURNEY

by Howard Nelson

"NOTICE: Big game season is now in effect. The wearing of
furs and hats with horns is not recommended, nor are any
dark colors—i.e., black, brown, gray."

> —trailhead warning, New York State
> Department of Environmental Conservation

I am wearing my gray wool pants, and my brown boots.
I set my name down in the trailhead register—
just past dawn, no one else around,
a few flakes of early snow
falling through the gray air.
And my black, water-repellent coat,
and my dark brown fur vest, buffalo fur,
and my Russian hat.
I will hike up to Avalanche Pass today,
and perhaps beyond,
at times sitting down on a rock
to listen to the silence or the wind,
and possibly the sound
of not so distant gunfire.
In my small black pack
I am carrying some dried fruit and nuts
and a canteen of water.
It's the only sensible thing to do.

We will see what happens.
I will breathe the cold air
and breathe out steam,
a dark figure striding among the birch woods.
I have always wanted to make this journey. Now
I strap on my nine-pronged antlers
and set off down the trail.

■ ■ ■

JADE'S IGUANAS ARE DEAD

by Gregory Razran

I'm on the phone with Jade.
She's washing her dishes;
I'm popping hazelnuts.
My sounds mix with hers:
Shells cracking; water running.
Jade's iguanas are dead,
And she is telling me about it.
I just had a feeling that morning,
She says, I got up . . . and everything
Felt so heavy. I don't know what to say
To that. I try to feel what she must've felt,
But the hazelnuts break my concentration.
They were lying side by side, like they knew,
She says, these two little dry green things.
Like iguana jerky, I say, and laugh out loud.
You asshole, she says, I'm hanging up.
And then she starts laughing, hysterically.
I hear her drop a dish back into the suds.
I picture her soapy pale hands on her hips;
The phone is caught between her head
And her left shoulder; Beautiful.
Thanks, man, she finally says, I needed that.

You got it, I say; We hang up.
That night, as I lie in bed, thoughts pop in and out.
Suddenly, I see it clearly: millions of iguanas, heaven-bound;
their little green souls fleeing their dry little bodies,
Flying far, far and away, the true lounge lizards.

■ ■ ■

RÉSUMÉ

by Dorothy Parker

Razors pain you;
Rivers are damp;
Acids stain you;
And drugs cause cramp.
Guns aren't lawful;
Nooses give;
Gas smells awful;
You might as well live.

■ ■ ■

I THINK I'LL CALL IT MORNING

by Gil Scott-Heron

I'm gonna take myself a piece of sunshine
and paint it all over my sky.
Be no rain. Be no rain.
I'm gonna take the song from every bird
and make them sing it just for me.
Be no rain.
And I think I'll call it morning from now on.
Why should I survive on sadness
convince myself I've got to be alone?
Why should I subscribe to this world's
            madness
knowing that I've got to live on?

I think I'll call it morning from now on.
I'm gonna take myself a piece of sunshine
and paint it all over my sky.
Be no rain. Be no rain.
I'm gonna take the song from every bird
and make them sing it just for me.
Why should I hang my head?
Why should I let tears fall from my eyes
when I've seen everything that there is to see
and I know that there ain't no sense in crying!
        I know that there ain't no sense in crying!
I think I'll call it morning from now on.

■ ■ ■

From DEATH'S ECHO

by W. H. Auden

The desires of the heart are as crooked as corkscrews
    Not to be born is the best for man
The second best is a formal order
    The dance's pattern, dance while you can.
Dance, dance, for the figure is easy
    The tune is catching and will not stop
Dance till the stars come down with the rafters
    Dance, dance, dance till you drop.

■■■

KINDNESS

by Naomi Shihab Nye

Before you know what kindness really is
you must lose things, feel the future dissolve in a moment
like salt in a weakened broth.
What you held in your hand,
what you counted and carefully saved,
all this must go so you know
how desolate the landscape can be
between the regions of kindness.
How you ride and ride
thinking the bus will never stop,
the passengers eating maize and chicken
will stare out the window forever.

Before you learn the tender gravity of kindness,
you must travel where the
Indian in a white poncho lies dead
by the side of the road.
You must see how this could be you, how he too was
        someone who journeyed through the night
with plans and the simple breath
that kept him alive.

Before you know kindness
as the deepest thing inside,
you must know sorrow
as the other deepest thing.

You must wake up with sorrow.
You must speak to it till your voice
catches the thread of all sorrows
and you see the size of the cloth.
Then it is only kindness
that makes sense anymore,
only kindness that ties your shoes
and sends you out into the day
to mail letters and purchase bread,
only kindness that raises its head
from the crowd of the world to say
it is I you have been looking for,
and then goes with you everywhere
like a shadow or a friend.

■ ■ ■

THE SNOW MAN

by Wallace Stevens

One must have a mind of winter
To regard the frost and the boughs
Of the pine-trees crusted with snow;

And have been cold a long time
To behold the junipers shagged with ice,
The spruces rough in the distant glitter

Of the January sun; and not to think
Of any misery in the sound of the wind,
In the sound of a few leaves,

Which is the sound of the land
Full of the same wind
That is blowing in the same bare place

For the listener, who listens in the snow,
And, nothing himself, beholds
Nothing that is not there and the nothing that is.

■ ■ ■

From THE PRISONER: A FRAGMENT

by Emily Brontë

"Still, let my tyrants know, I am not doomed to wear
Year after year in gloom and desolate despair;
A messenger of Hope comes every night to me,
And offers, for short life, eternal liberty.

"He comes with western winds, with evening's wandering
      airs,
With that clear dusk of heaven that brings the thickest stars;
Winds take a pensive tone, and stars a tender fire,
And visions rise and change that kill me with desire—

"Desire for nothing known in my maturer years
When joy grew mad with awe at counting future tears;
When, if my spirit's sky was full of flashes warm,
I knew not whence they came, from sun or thunderstorm;

"But first a hush of peace, a soundless calm descends;
The struggle of distress and fierce impatience ends;
Mute music soothes my breast—unuttered harmony
That I could never dream till earth was lost to me.

"Then dawns the Invisible, the Unseen its truth reveals;
My outward sense is gone, my inward essence feels—
Its wings are almost free, its home, its harbour found;
Measuring the gulf it stoops and dares the final bound!

"Oh, dreadful is the check—intense the agony
When the ear begins to hear and the eye begins to see;
When the pulse begins to throb, the brain to think again,
The soul to feel the flesh and the flesh to feel the chain!

"Yet I would lose no sting, would wish no torture less;
The more than anguish racks the earlier it will bless;
And robed in fires of Hell, or bright with heavenly shine,
If it but herald Death, the vision is divine."

She ceased to speak, and we, unanswering turned to go—
We had no further power to work the captive woe;
Her cheek, her gleaming eye, declared that man had given
A sentence unapproved, and overruled by Heaven.

■ ■ ■

A GLASS OF WATER

by May Sarton

Here is a glass of water from my well.
It tastes of rock and root and earth and rain;
It is the best I have, my only spell,
And it is cold, and better than champagne.
Perhaps someone will pass this house one day
To drink, and be restored, and go his way,
Someone in dark confusion as I was
When I drank down cold water in a glass,
Drank a transparent health to keep me sane,
After the bitter mood had gone again.

■ ■ ■

HOW A PLACE BECOMES HOLY

by Yehoshua November

Sometimes a man
will start crying in the middle of the street,
without knowing why or for whom.
It is as though someone else is standing
there, holding his briefcase, wearing his coat.

And from beneath the rust of years,
come to his tongue the words of his childhood.
"G-d" and "I'm sorry," and "Do not be far from me."

And just as suddenly the tears are gone,
and the man walks back into his life,
and the place where he cried becomes holy.

■ ■ ■

SUNFLOWER

by Rolf Jacobsen
Translated by Olav Grinde

What sower has walked over the Earth,
what hands have sown
our inner seeds of fire?

Like rainbow curves they went out from his hands
to frozen earth, young loam, hot sand.
There they shall sleep
greedily and drink our life
and blast it to pieces
for the sake of a sunflower you don't know,
or a thistle crown or a chrysanthemum.

Let the young rain of tears come;
let the mild hands of grief come.
It's not as terrible as you think.

■ ■ ■

LATE FRAGMENT

by Raymond Carver

And did you get what
you wanted from this life, even so?
I did.
And what did you want?
To call myself beloved, to feel myself
beloved on the earth.

■ ■ ■

EVIL TIME

by Hermann Hesse

Translated by James Wright

Now we are silent
And sing no songs any more,
Our pace grows heavy;
This is the night, that was bound to come.

Give me your hand,
Perhaps we still have a long way to go.
It's snowing, it's snowing.
Winter is a hard thing in a strange country.

Where is the time
When a light, a hearth burned for us?
Give me your hand!
Perhaps we still have a long way to go.

■ ■ ■

"FOR YEARS, COPYING OTHER PEOPLE, I TRIED TO KNOW MYSELF"

by Rumi

Translated by Coleman Barks

For years, copying other people, I tried to know myself.
From within, I couldn't decide what to do.
Unable to see, I heard my name being called.
Then I walked outside.

■ ■ ■

BIOGRAPHIES

FLEUR ADCOCK was born in Auckland, New Zealand, but spent most of her childhood in England. She began writing poems at the age of five. In 1963, she moved to London, where she worked as a librarian at the Foreign and Commonwealth Office. In addition to writing poetry, she has been an editor and translator, and has written song-cycles and a full-length opera. Her poetry has received numerous awards, including a Cholmondeley Award, a Buckland Award, and an OBE.

ANTLER is a Milwaukee poet laureate who spends weeks at a time alone in the wilderness. He was born and raised in Wauwatosa, Wisconsin, and earned a bachelor's degree in anthropology and a master's degree in English from the University of Wisconsin-Milwaukee. His work is widely published and anthologized; his most recent book is his *Selected Poems* from Soft Skull Press. Antler, who was given his name as a teenager, has said that his inspiration to write comes from "human beauty and the beauty of the natural world."

MARGARET ATWOOD is a Canadian author of more than twenty volumes of poetry in addition to highly prized and best-selling works of fiction and nonfiction. Her novel *The Blind Assassin* won the 2000 Booker Prize. Atwood graduated from Victoria College at the University of Toronto and earned her master's degree from Radcliffe College. She currently resides in Toronto with her husband, Graeme Gibson.

W. H. AUDEN (1907–1973) was born in York, England, the son of a physician. At first interested in science, philosophy, and politics, he turned to writing poetry and attended Oxford, where he met a group of like-minded writers. In 1937, he drove an ambulance for the Loyalists in the Spanish civil war. That same year he won the King's Gold Medal for Poetry. He was a socialist, a Christian, an editor, an essayist, a librettist, and one of the most important literary figures of the twentieth century. He struggled with his own homosexuality, at that time considered a crime. Auden traveled around the world before moving to the United States in 1939 with his young lover and becoming an American citizen. He won many prizes and honors, including the Pulitzer Prize for poetry for *The Age of Anxiety*.

CHARLES BAUDELAIRE (1821–1867) was born in Paris to a respected, well-to-do family. He was expelled from school, and only under pressure from his family agreed to study law. He published poems, novels, and essays on art, and translated into French the works of Edgar Allen Poe. His collection of prose poems, *Paris Spleen*, was published only after his death. Baudelaire is considered one of the founders of the French Symbolist Movement, whose followers, such as Verlaine and Rimbaud, sought to "derange" meaning and to write about gritty urban life, as well as the life of images and dreams.

OSCAR BERMEO was born in Ecuador and raised in the Bronx. He is the founding curator and host of the Acentos Bronx Poetry Showcase, a founder of the synonymUS experimental poetry workshop, a member of the louderARTS Project, and a BRIO (Bronx Recognizes Its Own) award-winning poet. He has facilitated poetry workshops at Rikers Island and represented louderARTS at the SlamMasters Slam in Chicago, and his work appears in several anthologies. Currently, Bermeo teaches creative writing to teenagers in the Bronx by day and is an avid listener and frequent reader at poetry venues in New York City by night.

JOHN BERRYMAN (1914–1972) was born John Smith in MacAlester, Oklahoma. His father committed suicide in 1926, and Berryman first attempted suicide while he was in his twenties. He attended Columbia and later won a fellowship to Cambridge University; he taught at Harvard, Princeton, and for nearly twenty years at the University of Minnesota. His book *77 Dream Songs* was published in 1964 and won the Pulitzer Prize. In it he invents the poetic characters "Henry" and "Mr. Bones"; he later added more poems to the sequence until there were nearly four hundred poems collected as *The Dream Songs*. Through his life he suffered from alcoholism and repeated nervous breakdowns. He committed suicide in 1972.

ELIZABETH BISHOP (1911–1979) was born in Worcester, Massachusetts, but spent much of her childhood with her Canadian grandparents after her father's death and her mother's permanent hospitalization in a Nova Scotia sanitarium. Bishop traveled all over the world and lived for sixteen years in a pink house in Brazil. Her work won the Pulitzer Prize, two Guggenheim Fellowships, the National Book Award, and the National Book Critics Circle Award. In addition to writing poetry and prose and painting, she also translated a famous Brazilian diary, *The Diary of Helena Morley*, and coedited and cotranslated *An Anthology of Contemporary Brazilian Poetry*. She served as chancellor of the Academy of American Poets and consultant in poetry to the Library of Congress in 1949–1950 (an earlier name for the current post of U.S. poet laureate). Her posthumous works include *The Complete Poems, 1927–1979* (1983) and *The Collected Prose* (1984).

WILLIAM BLAKE (1757–1827) was a visionary even as a child—he claimed he saw angels in the tree by his childhood house, and he continued to see and communicate with them all his life. Blake began writing poetry when he was twelve, and at fourteen became apprenticed to an engraver. He studied briefly at the British Royal Academy but rebelled against the doctrines of its president, Sir Joshua Reynolds. He eked out a living as an engraver and illustrator, and illustrated many of his own poems. He suffered from what he called the "Deep pit of Melancholy" but signed his letters "Enthusiastic, hope-fostered visionary." He wrote short, cryptic poems as well as epics, satires, letters, and commentaries. Blake continued to speak to his wife, Katharine, in their garden after his death—or so she claimed. Needless to say, they were beautifully matched. He embraced his own moods and visions in lines like "Excess of sorrow laughs. Excess of joy weeps" and "If the fool would persist in his folly he would become wise."

ELI BOSNICK is a high school student living in upstate New York. His great passion in life is acting, though his original ambition at age four was to be a gravedigger. He sometimes feels sadness without reason, but most of the time he is excited about life. He has been writing poems and stories since age seven.

EMILY BRONTË (1818–1848) was an English Victorian poet and novelist born to a family of writers and artists, including sister Charlotte Brontë, the author of *Jane Eyre*. When Emily was two years old, her mother died, and at age six she lost two of her elder sisters as well. Emily is most famous for her powerfully eerie and romantic novel *Wuthering Heights*. In May of 1848, her brother Branwell died after suffering from drug addiction and alcoholism, and later that year, in December, Emily died from consumption, a year after her novel's publication.

CHARLES BUKOWSKI (1920–1994) is a well-known contemporary writer of poetry and prose. Born in Andernach, Germany, he came to the United States at the age of three. Raised in Los Angeles, where he lived for fifty years, he started out poor and abused, and later became an alcoholic. He worked many odd jobs and in 1955 he began writing poetry. Though his first collection, *Power, Fist, and Bestial Wail*, was published in 1959, it took a long time for him to become widely published. Bukowski died in 1994 after completing his final novel, *Pulp* (1994). He wrote forty-five books of poetry and prose, some which are *Burning in Water, Drowning in Flame: Selected Poems 1955–1973* (1974), *Love Is a Dog from Hell: Poems 1974–1977* (1977), *Bone Palace Ballet: New Poems* (1997), and *The Night Torn Mad with Footsteps: New Poems* (2001).

MICHAEL BURKARD has published four collections of poetry, as well as *My Secret Boat, A Notebook of Prose and Poems*. He has received a Whiting Writers' Award, the Poetry Society of America's Alice Fay di Castagnola Award, and grants from the New York State Foundation for the Arts and the National Endowment for the Arts. During the 1990s, he worked as an alcoholism counselor, particularly with children whose lives were affected by alcoholism. He teaches at Syracuse University.

GEORGE GORDON, LORD BYRON (1788–1823) acquired the title of baron at age ten, when a great-uncle died, leaving him a castle. He lived a short, dramatic, often famous and scandalous life, and despite his clubfoot was quite the ladies' man. A woman friend wrote that he was "mad, bad, and dangerous to know." The first two cantos of his long poem *Childe Harold* sold out within days of publication, and he commented, "I awoke one morning and found myself famous." He died while helping to fight for Greece's independence and became an immediate Greek national hero—but his body was refused burial at Westminster Abbey until one hundred and fifty years after his death.

LEWIS CARROLL (1832–1898) was born Charles Lutwidge Dodgson in Daresbury, Cheshire, England, the son of a clergyman, and one of eleven children. From a very early age, he entertained himself and his family by performing magic tricks and marionette shows, and by writing poetry for his homemade newspapers. He graduated from Christ Church College, Oxford, in mathematics and writing, and remained at Oxford after graduation to teach. His mathematical writings are well known, but he is most famous for two children's books: *Alice's*

Adventures in Wonderland and *Through the Looking Glass*. The poem "You Are Old, Father William," from *Alice's Adventures in Wonderland* was written partly as a satire of the poet William Wordsworth.

RAYMOND CARVER (1938–1988) is best known as a short story writer. He struggled for many years without recognition before his work became known and published, and widely prized. He was born in Clatskanie, Oregon, a mill town on the Columbia River. His father was an alcoholic, and the family struggled to get by. Carver became interested in writing in California, where he studied with the novelist John Gardner. Though he struggled in his life with a failed early first marriage, alcoholism, and depression, he ended feeling both happy and blessed. Carver lived much of the last ten years of his life with his wife, the poet and author Tess Gallagher, in Port Angeles, Washington. Carver's reputation continued to grow after his death. Robert Altman's much-praised film *Short Cuts* (1993) was based on several of Carver's stories.

SAMUEL TAYLOR COLERIDGE (1772–1834) was one of the first and most eloquent of the British Romantic poets. He wrote short lyrics, long narratives, political commentary, and criticism. According to contemporaries, his spontaneous conversation was brilliant and unreproducable. Someone compared him to "a glow-worm with a pin stuck thro' it"; a friend described him as "an Arch angel a little damaged" and he suffered greatly—from childhood illness and the early death of his father; from poverty and difficult romances, a troubled marriage, depression, agonizing stomach ailments and neuralgia, and subsequent addiction to opium. His friendship with the poet William Wordsworth was a turning point in his life—by turns elevating, productive, and disappointing. He left behind less than he might have had he not struggled with so many demons, but among his most famous works are "The Rime of the Ancient Mariner," "Kubla Khan," and his Biographia Literaria.

WILLIAM COWPER (1731–1800) was an English poet and translator. He wrote during the Restoration period and was a nonconformist. Periodically insane, Cowper attempted suicide because he felt damned and cast away from God. In order to divert his depression, he wrote. He collaborated on Olney Hymns with the Reverend John Newton. His poems include The Task and John Gilpin's Ride.

STEPHEN CRANE (1871–1900) was born in Newark, New Jersey, the fourteenth child of a Methodist minister. He wrote journalism, stories, poems, and novels, the most famous of which is The Red Badge of Courage, a grippingly convincing story about war, though Crane himself had never witnessed a battle. As a result of writing that book, however, he began a career as a war correspondent, whose assignments took him to Cuba, Greece, and Turkey. He died of tuberculosis before he was thirty.

ALVIN DELGADO teaches seventh grade English. He was born in Puerto Rico and lives in Binghamton, New York. He has written several stories for young readers and he enjoys playing tennis and fishing with his wife and children. He is at work on a novel for young adults.

EMILY DICKINSON (1830–1886) was a New England poet who never married and seldom left her house after she reached adulthood. Toward the end of her life, she would not admit visitors upstairs to see her, but occasionally left the door open if she wanted to hear their conversation. Many famous authors were well known to Dickinson, including the poet and essayist Ralph Waldo Emerson. She was widely read, had a few close, passionate friendships, and loved her dog, Carlo, and the natural world. She chose never to publish her poems, instead sewing them into carefully made portfolios, which she kept in her drawer at home. Readers and critics still debate whether Emily Dickinson was simply divinely stubborn and reclusive or suffered from mental illness.

STEPHEN DOBYNS has published ten books of poems, a book of essays on poetry called *Best Words, Best Order*, and more than twenty highly successful mystery novels, two of which have been made into films. Dobyns earned his M.F.A. from the writing program at the University of Iowa. He became a reporter for the *Detroit News* in 1969, and has taught at numerous universities and colleges.

TWAIN DOOLEY grew up in Washington, D.C., where he has been writing and performing poetry for more than ten years. Twain has been a member of the D.C./Baltimore Slam Team for five consecutive years. He currently lives in the suburbs with his wife, fellow poet Gayle Danley.

PAUL LAURENCE DUNBAR (1872–1906), poet and novelist, was born in Dayton, Ohio, the son of a former slave. He edited his high school paper and then worked for a time as an elevator operator. He published his first book of poems, *Oak and Ivy*, at his own expense, and his second, *Majors and Minors*, two years later. After his third book, *Lyrics of Lowly Life*, Dunbar's work had gained enough recognition and popular acclaim to enable him to earn his living as a writer.

T. S. ELIOT (1888–1965) was born in St. Louis, Missouri, educated at Harvard, and did graduate work in philosophy at the Sorbonne, Harvard, and Oxford. He later worked as a teacher, as a bank clerk, and for the publishing house Faber & Faber as a literary editor, later becoming a director. He also founded and edited the influential literary journal *Criterion*. In 1927, Eliot became a British citizen and about the same time entered the Anglican Church. In addition to poetry, he wrote criticism and plays.

THOMAS SCOTT FISKEN, called Scott by family and friends, is nineteen years old and lives in Highland Park, New Jersey. He has autism and communicates and writes with computers. He attended Highland Park High School. Fiskin won first place in the Rutgers Newark High School Poetry Contest and in the nonfiction category of the New Jersey Council of Teachers of English High School Writing Contest. He also received the New Jersey Governor's Arts Award. Fiskin has taken gymnastics lessons for twelve years and is on Special Olympics teams in cycling and bowling. Still, he finds time to sit on his front porch, watching the Highland Park scene.

SUSAN LOVE FITTS was born in Natchez, Mississippi, and grew up in a large family. Fitts now lives in Texas, where she is a freelance writer published in many Texas newspapers, and organizes poetry readings and open mic events.

ANGELINA WELD GRIMKÈ (1880–1958), a writer and poet of the Black Renaissance in Washington, D.C., was the daughter of a prominent black clergyman who was an influential lawyer, diplomat, author, editor, and publisher, as well as vice president of the NAACP. Her mother was a white woman whose parents strongly disapproved the match, and she abandoned the family when Angelina was a child. The poet was named after her famous aunt, Angelina Grimkè Weld, an abolitionist and a suffragist for women's rights. Angelina wrote poems and plays and taught English in Washington, D.C.

HERMANN HESSE (1877–1962) was a German poet and novelist born to pious missionary parents who expected him to follow in their footsteps. Though Hesse entered a Protestant seminary in 1891, he was soon expelled. He worked as a bookshop clerk, a mechanic, and a book dealer in Tübingen. During this period Hesse read avidly and found writing as his true vocation: "It will become evident that formulations in words and the handing on of these formulations through writing are not only important aids but actually the only means by which humanity can have a history and continuing consciousness of itself" (*Reading in Bed*). During World War I, Hesse spoke out against militarism and nationalism. He promoted the interests of prisoners of war. He was three times married and divorced, and his fourth marriage was to a Jewish woman. This, in addition to his outspoken criticism of Nazi persecutions, led him to be placed on the Nazi blacklist in 1943. Hesse was awarded the Nobel Prize for Literature in 1946. He became a cult figure in the 1960s for novels such as *Siddhartha, Demian,* and *Steppenwolf.*

IKKYŪ (1394–1481) was born in Kyoto, Japan, the natural child of Emperor Go Komatsu and a favorite lady in waiting. By the age of thirteen, Ikkyū was composing a poem a day in Chinese. By age fifteen his poems were already well known and widely recited. He became a Zen monk, poet, calligrapher, and musician. He was a renegade almost all his life. Appointed headmaster at a great temple in Kyoto, Ikkyū lasted nine days before he was kicked out for denouncing the hypocrisy among the monks. He lived during harsh times in Japan, times of war, famine, and religious upheavals. A fuller biography by his translator Stephen Berg appears in the book *Crow with No Mouth: Ikkyū.*

ROLF JACOBSEN (1907–1994) was born in Oslo, Norway. Rolf was taught at home by his mother, but in 1920 he entered a private school under the care of his uncle. Jacobson continued his studies at the University of Oslo for five years without graduating. He served briefly in the Norwegian army. Jacobsen's career as a writer spanned more than fifty years as journalist and poet, including sixteen years during which he wrote no poetry. During the Nazi occupation of Norway, Jacobsen signed and published editorials that supported the German occupiers. When Norway was again free, Jacobsen was convicted of treason and sentenced to three and a half years of hard labor. In 1950, he converted to Catholicism and began writing more traditional verse. His work won numerous honors and awards, including the Swedish Academy's Dobloug Prize and the Grand Nordic Prize, also known as the "Little Nobel"; the Norwegian Critics Award in 1960; and the Aschehoug Award in 1986.

LOUIS JENKINS was born in Oklahoma City and has lived in Duluth, Minnesota, for almost thirty years. Jenkins finds walking to be helpful in developing his writing ideas. As he walks he composes poetry in his head and then returns home to type. About writing poetry, he states, "It's what I do. If I could do something else better, I'd do that. But I can't." Jenkins is author to several books including *Nice Fish: New and Selected Prose Poems* (1995), *Just Above Water* (1997), and *The Winter Road* (2000).

JUNE JORDAN (1936–2002) was born in Harlem, New York, the child of a night-shift postal worker and a nurse. Her home life was troubled: her father was often violent, and she felt that in high school she was black in a "white world." In 1953, Jordan enrolled at Barnard College. Two years later, she married Michael Meyer, a white student, and together they had a son. In 1969, Jordan published her first book of poetry, *Who Look at Me*, which dealt with the struggles and truths of African-American life. She also worked as a research associate and writer for the Technical Housing Department of Mobilization for Youth in New York and taught at numerous colleges and universities. Her first novel, *His Own Where*, was nominated for the National Book Award. She wrote children's books, essays, songs, opera libretti, and speeches. Jordan received numerous honors and awards, including a Rockefeller grant, a National Endowment for the Arts fellowship, the Ground Breakers—Dream Makers award, and the PEN Center USA West Freedom to Write Award, 1991. Jordan died of breast cancer in 2002.

JOHN KEATS (1795–1818), an English poet, died at age twenty-four of tuberculosis, then known as consumption. Keats left behind a few long poems and some of the most exquisite odes ever written in the English language. His father died when he was nine and his mother when Keats was fifteen. By the time he was sixteen he had been apprenticed to a surgeon and apothecary, though he showed an early love and gift for poetry. In a letter to his brother George he wrote: "Do you not see how necessary a World of pains and troubles is to school an Intelligence and make it a Soul?" His books were scorned by contemporary critics, and he died believing he was a failure as a poet. He composed his own epitaph, which read, "Here lies one whose name was writ in water."

JANE KENYON (1947–1995) was born in Ann Arbor, Michigan, and attended the University of Michigan. She later married a teacher at the university, the poet Donald Hall. After their marriage, they moved to Eagle Pond Farm in New Hampshire, which had been Hall's family home for generations. Kenyon suffered from severe depression throughout her life, and her poetry bravely documents that long struggle. Her first book, Let Evening Come, was published in 1990. Jane Kenyon and Donald Hall were the subject of a Bill Moyers PBS documentary that depicted their shared life of poetry. Jane Kenyon died of leukemia in 1995.

DAS LANZILLOTI was born in Pennsylvania and raised in a rural community in New Jersey, where his best friends were the cows. He found himself in New York City after high school, and a confrontation with the police led to admission to a mental asylum. There, he witnessed helpless, innocent people subjected daily to injustice. He decided to reform the mental health program in America — a virtually impossible undertaking — and finally decided to say what he felt were the right things to the evaluation board to get released. He has been insanity-free for many years but still has memories of the asylum. He married early, had two children, divorced, and has been a political activist, artist, jewelry maker, and writer since. He splits his time between Sarasota, Florida, and a quiet part of the Chihuahua desert in New Mexico.

D. H. LAWRENCE (1885–1930), born David Herbert Lawrence, was a poet, novelist, essayist and painter. He is perhaps most famous for his novel *Lady Chatterly's Lover*, which was banned as obscene and nearly got Lawrence jailed. He was born and raised in Nottingshire, England, the fourth of five children of a hard-working coal miner and his wife. During his adult life, Lawrence lived all over the world, including Ceylon, Australia, and New Mexico.

J. PATRICK LEWIS has published more than twenty-five books for children, seventeen of them children's poetry, yet was trained in economics at Ohio State University (1974). In

1972–1973, his family spent the academic year in Russia, where Lewis completed his doctoral dissertation as an International Research and Exchanges (IREX) Fellow. Lewis was commissioned to write the 1992 National Children's Book Week poem, printed on one million bookmarks and distributed throughout the United States. His work has appeared in numerous magazines and journals, and in more than sixty anthologies.

AMY LOWELL (1874–1925) was born to the famous and powerful Boston Lowell family. (See Robert Lowell.) She and the poet Ezra Pound formed a school of poets known as the Imagists, which he later nicknamed "the Amy-gists." She wrote poetry, criticism, and biography. Her life and work were virtually forgotten until the second wave of the women's movement rediscovered her poems. T. S. Eliot called her the "demon saleswoman of poetry." Of herself, she said, "God made me a businesswoman and I made myself a poet."

ROBERT LOWELL (1917–1977) was born in Boston, Massachusetts, and attended Harvard University, in the Lowell family tradition. But Robert left Harvard after two years, transferring to Kenyon College to study poetry. He won the Pulitzer Prize in 1947 for his first book of poems, and again in 1974. Lowell was a conscientious objector during World War II. He suffered from manic depression throughout his life. He is considered the father of confessional poetry, a personal and rawly honest form of writing. Both Sylvia Plath and Anne Sexton were his students.

HOWARD NELSON writes poems and essays in Scipio, New York, in the Finger Lakes region, where he also teaches. His books of poems include *Gorilla Blessing* and *Bone Music*. He frequently publishes essays on poets and poetry in the *Hollins Critic*.

DEENA NOVEMBER was born in Kansas City, Missouri, and began writing poetry at age fourteen. She studied creative writing at the State University of New York at Binghamton and finds inspiration on the city bus, but tells strangers her "problems" too often. Occasionally, she writes for the online magazine 1-42.

YEHOSHUA NOVEMBER lives with his wife and daughter in Morristown, New Jersey, where he attends the Rabbinical College of America. He studied poetry at Binghamton University and earned his M.F.A. in Creative Writing at the University of Pittsburgh. He plans to teach Judaic studies and English.

NAOMI SHIHAB NYE was born in St. Louis, Missouri, to an American mother and a Palestinian father. At seven, she published her first poem and when she was fourteen her family moved to Jerusalem, where she attended a year of high school. After earning her B.A., Naomi Shihab Nye began her career as a freelance writer, editor, and speaker. She has earned numerous awards for her writing, including four Pushcart Prizes, the Jane Addams Children's Book Award, the Paterson Poetry Prize, and many Notable Book and Best Book citations from the American Library Association. She has edited five prizewinning anthologies of poetry for young readers, as well as writing her own books of poems, a novel, and a picture book.

DOROTHY PARKER (1883–1967) was a poet, critic, playwright, and short story writer. Born in West End, New Jersey, Parker was four when her mother died. Her brother died on the *Titanic* and her father passed away before she was twenty. She wrote for *Vogue*, *Vanity Fair*, *The New Yorker*, and *Life*. Parker drank heavily and attempted suicide three times. She died alone in her hotel room at the age of seventy-four. She left her estate to the NAACP.

SYLVIA PLATH (1932–1963) published her first poem at age eight, the year her father died. She attended Smith College and won a Fulbright scholarship to study in Cambridge, England, where she met her future husband, the British poet Ted Hughes. Plath was a prolific poet and author, but her famous novel, *The Bell Jar*, was first published under a pseudonym, and her most famous poems were published posthumously, following her suicide at age thirty. She suffered from deep depression throughout her short, brilliant life. She was a student of Robert Lowell's and a friend of Anne Sexton's.

EDGAR ALLEN POE (1809–1849) was born in Boston and raised in Virginia. His parents, both touring actors, died before Poe was three years old. Given to wild moods and melancholia, he was sent to and released from the army, then appointed to West Point, where he was expelled for refusing to obey orders. His fellow military men, however, pooled their money in order to publish a book of his poems. He married his cousin Virginia when she was thirteen years old, and her early death was a blow to him. Poe wrote poems, stories, tales, novellas, philosophy, and criticism—including reviews of his own books, which he would publish under a pseudonym. Poe died in a hospital after being found wandering the streets of Baltimore, Maryland. The circumstances of his dementia and death are still a mystery, although likely alcohol related.

GREGORY RAZRAN was born and raised in St. Petersburg, Russia. He came to the United States in 1992 and is currently a Ph.D. candidate at the State University of New York at Binghamton. For the past five years, he has been teaching American literature, creative writing, and Russian literature. His current and forthcoming publications include two chapbooks of poems and individual pieces in *Poems and Plays*, the *Paterson Review*, *Concrete Wolf*, and *Cross-Cultural Communications*.

ELAINE RESTIFO is a renegade senior citizen who cares passionately about social justice. She's a painter and a poet, and has been editing and publishing the periodical the *River* since 1969.

EDWIN ARLINGTON ROBINSON (1869–1935) grew up in a small town on the Kennebec River in Maine, the youngest of three brothers. His father was a well-to-do shipping merchant. Robinson began writing poetry at age eleven. He attended Harvard for two years but left when the family business ran aground. Soon after, Robinson's father died, and not long after that, his mother died as well. Robinson moved to New York City, where he lived in poverty, and began to publish his poetry, mostly with the help of friends. Robinson was working inspecting underground construction when President Theodore Roosevelt discovered his poetry. Roosevelt helped Robinson to get a clerkship in the New York City Customs House—the same politically appointed position once held by author Nathaniel Hawthorne. Robinson won the Pulitzer Prize three times. Though sometimes scorned by academics, his work remains popular with the American people.

THEODORE ROETHKE (1908–1963) was born in Saginaw, Michigan, and as a child spent a great deal of time in the family-owned greenhouse. He attended the University of Michigan and took a few classes at Harvard, but was unhappy in school. Roethke's father died when the poet was still a teenager. Later in life Roethke suffered numerous breakdowns and was diagnosed with manic-depressive illness. His first book, Open House (1941), took ten years to write. A later book, The Waking, won the Pulitzer Prize in 1954. Roethke also wrote essays, and his notebooks make wonderful reading as well. Roethke was a strict and beloved teacher, who used to give final exams in his writing classes that involved writing in complicated rhythms and forms.

LIZ ROSENBERG was born and raised on Long Island. She graduated from Bennington College, then Johns Hopkins, and has taught English and creative writing at the State University of New York at Binghamton since 1979. She has won the Chancellor's Award for Excellence in Undergraduate Teaching, the Agnet Starrett Poetry Prize, and the Lee Bennett

Hopkins Award, among other honors, and is the author of three books of poems, two novels, and more than twenty books for young readers. She has struggled with depression much of her life, but she and her husband live joyfully with their son and daughter and two dogs in Binghamton, N.Y.

MARY RUEFLE is the recipient of a National Endowment for the Arts fellowship, an American Academy of Arts and Letters Award in Literature, and a Whiting Foundation Writer's Award. Ruefle has published seven books of poetry. She lives in Massachusetts and is a professor at the Vermont College M.F.A. program.

JELALUDDIN RUMI (1207–1273) was born in what is now Afghanistan. Under threat of the Mongol invasion, Rumi and his family moved to Turkey. Rumi became a professor of religious sciences at twenty-four, following in the family tradition of scholars, theologians, and jurists. He was introduced to mysticism and to love by a wandering dervish, Shams of Tabriz, and it changed him forever. The night of Rumi's death is called The Night of Union, and Mawlawi dervishes have kept that date as a festival ever since. The poet Coleman Barks's translations of Rumi's poems—which Rumi composed and recited orally, with dance and with music—have become some of the most often read poems in the United States and were the subject of two Bill Moyers PBS specials.

MAY SARTON (1912–1995) was born in Belgium, but her family moved to the United States when she was four. Her father was the science historian George Sarton. May Sarton had an unhappy and often neglected childhood, but she became an immensely prolific author, publishing fifteen books of poetry, nineteen novels, and thirteen memoirs. She spent much of her life traveling between the United States and Europe, and had intense friendships and romances with some of the most interesting artists and writers of her time. She chronicled both her health and illnesses, her happiness and unhappiness, in autobiographical writings, journals, and letters.

KATE SCHMITT earned her bachelor's degree from Colgate University and her M.F.A. from the University of Houston's creative writing program. Her poems are often informed by her struggle with manic depression. She currently lives in Houston and is working on a Ph.D. in literature and creative writing.

GIL SCOTT-HERON is a writer, poet, composer, and pianist. He received a master's in creative writing from Johns Hopkins. Scott-Heron emerged in the seventies as a strong civil rights activist and radical rap musician with a political message of equality.

ANNE SEXTON (1928–1974) was born in Newton, Massachusetts. She spent one year at Garland Junior College, a finishing school for women, and married Alfred Muller Sexton II at age nineteen. Sexton suffered a number of breakdowns during her life, two of them postpartum depressions following the birth of each of her two daughters. She was encouraged by her doctors to pursue her interest in poetry and in 1957 enrolled in a poetry workshop at the Boston Center for Adult

Education. Through her studies in poetry, she met Maxine Kumin, Robert Lowell, and others. Sexton won the Pulitzer Prize for poetry in 1967 for her book *Live or Die*. Despite many successes and a career as poet, playwright, children's book writer, and performer of her own poetry, Sexton committed suicide in 1974 and is buried near her friend Sylvia Plath's birthplace, in Jamaica Plain, Massachusetts.

WILLIAM SHAKESPEARE (1554–1616) is probably the most famous and brilliant author ever to have written in the English language. Despite that fact, we still know relatively little about his life. He was born in Stratford, England, and left for London as a teenager to pursue a career first as an actor and later as playwright and poet. He wrote two long poems, more than thirty-five plays, and more than one hundred and fifty sonnets. Many scholars believe that his love sonnets were written sometimes to a man, sometimes to a "dark lady." He was married to Anne Hathaway and left to her his "second-best bed."

STEVIE SMITH (1902–1971) was born Florence Margaret Smith in Hull, England, though she was always called Peggy. Her father ran away to sea when she was three, and her mother died when Stevie was sixteen. She worked as a secretary at a publishing house in London for thirty years, and occasionally as a writer and broadcaster for the BBC. In the 1950s, she attempted suicide, and shortly thereafter retired from secretarial work. In 1957 the collection *Not Waving but Drowning* appeared, and in 1958 a collection of her sketches, *Some Are More Human Than Others*, was published. In 1959 she wrote the text for the *Batsford Book of Cats in Colour* and edited the

Batsford Book of Children's Verse. Though she began publishing verse, which she often illustrated herself, in the 1930s, Smith did not reach a wide audience until 1962, with the publication of her *Selected Poems* and her appearance in the Penguin Modern Poets Series. Smith won the Queen's Gold Medal for poetry in 1969. She published three novels in addition to eight volumes of poetry.

GERALD STERN was born in Pittsburgh, Pennsylvania. His recent books of poetry include *Last Blue: Poems*, and *This Time: New and Selected Poems* (1998), which won the 1998 National Book Award. His other honors include the Ruth Lilly Prize, four National Endowment for the Arts grants, and fellowships from the Academy of American Poets, the Guggenheim Foundation, and the Pennsylvania Council on the Arts. Stern taught for many years at the Writers' Workshop in Iowa, as well as at Columbia, New York University, Sarah Lawrence College, and elsewhere. He lives in New Jersey and New York. In 2003 W. W. Norton published a collection of his personal essays, *What I Can't Bear Losing: Notes Toward a Life*.

WALLACE STEVENS (1879–1955) was born in Reading, Pennsylvania, and showed an early interest in and genius for writing. He attended Harvard for three years, studying French, German, and philosophy, and then began working as a journalist at the *New York Herald Tribune*. His father suggested he try his hand at law, but it didn't suit him any better than journalism. In 1916 he had begun working at the New York office of the Hartford Accident and Indemnification Company, and eventually became its vice president. He never spoke of his literary endeavors at work, and was by most accounts a quiet and conservative man. One of his most famous books of poems, Harmonium, was published in 1923, but the publication of T. S. Eliot's *The Waste Land* a year earlier seems to have overshadowed it, and his reputation grew slowly and steadily. He had a wife and a daughter, and claimed to have led a matter-of-fact, "quiet, normal" life, though poetry was, for him, "the supreme fiction."

CÉSAR VALLEJO (1892–1938), a Peruvian poet, was the youngest of eleven children. Both of his grandfathers were priests. Vallejo left the poor mining town where he was raised to go to college. When he returned home, he became involved in a local political feud that resulted in a three-month jail sentence and years of reprisals. Soon after his second book of poems was published, Vallejo lost his teaching job in Peru, and he went to live, often in the most dire poverty, in Paris, France. He became interested in politics, and in the rights of the poor and the downtrodden, and he desperately wanted to join the ranks of the Loyalist freedom fighters during the Spanish civil war. Instead, he took ill in Paris. He predicted he would die on a rainy day in Paris, which is exactly what he did, on Good Friday, in 1938.

DIETER WESLOWSKI writes: "As I am not one to sing about where my poems have or have not appeared, let it suffice to say that poetry has been the filtering station through which all the insanity of my life has passed on its way to something approximating mortal joy. Speaking of life, I now realize that it makes us up, not the other way 'round." He lives and works outside Boston, Massachusetts, and is the author of *The Bird Who Steals Everything Shining*.

WILLIAM WORDSWORTH (1770–1850) grew up in the rural English lake district. After studying at Cambridge University, he spent a tempestuous year in revolutionary France. Upon his return to England, he became close friends with the poet Samuel Taylor Coleridge and together they published a book of their poems called *Lyrical Ballads*. Coleridge became an opium addict and died early, while Wordsworth went on to become poet laureate and a stolid conservative. He is best known for his poems about nature and childhood, and is considered among the first of the Romantic poets.

JAMES WRIGHT (1927–1980) was born in Martins Ferry, Ohio. His father labored in the Hazel-Atlas Glass factory most of his life, a fate that James feared he was doomed to replicate. Wright missed a year of high school at age sixteen due to a nervous breakdown, and he suffered from manic depression throughout his life. He attended Kenyon College on the GI Bill, was elected to Phi Beta Kappa, and won the Robert Frost Poetry Prize. At the University of Washington, he studied under the poet Theodore Roethke. His poetry manuscript *The Green Wall* was selected for the Yale Series of Younger Poets Award. Wright taught at Hunter College in New York, where he met his second wife, Edith Ann Runk. They spent a number of summers in Italy and Paris, traveling and writing.

ELINOR WYLIE (1885–1928) was an American poet and novelist, born in New Jersey. Her father served as assistant U.S. attorney general and later as solicitor general. She was beautiful, glamorous, moody, and difficult. She ran away from her first marriage, creating a national scandal, divorced a second time, and abandoned the care of her only child to other family members. Her book of poems *Nets to Catch the Wind* was an immediate success when it was published in 1921. In 1922, Wylie became literary editor of *Vanity Fair*. She died of Bright's disease in 1928.

WILLIAM BUTLER YEATS (1865–1939) was a Nobel laureate and a leader in the Irish renaissance movement. He helped found the famous Abbey Theatre in Dublin and was interested in everything from myth to mysticism, the occult, Irish politics, and automatic writing. He married late, but the great love of his life was Maude Gonne, the fiery Irish nationalist, actress, and beauty whom he courted unsuccessfully for many years. He wrote poetry, stories, autobiography, plays, children's books, essays, and philosophy. He created a number of poems about the character "Crazy Jane" and, whether or not he was ever mad himself, had a keen understanding of the condition.

PERMISSIONS

INDEX OF AUTHORS

INDEX OF TITLES

INDEX OF FIRST LINES